Praise For "To Love and Be Cherished"

"In her book, "To Love and Be Cherished," Kirsten writes with a truly genuine and thoughtful voice. This book reads and flows as easily as two friends sharing meaningful conversation over coffee. It will leave you feeling inspired and empowered."
-MaryBeth Koberna, Friend, Mom and Survivor.

Kirsten has a natural gift from God in terms of being able to touch a person's inner-most feelings and emotions through her words. I sat down to read the manuscript thinking it would be a great read, but a read that would not apply to me being that I have been married for 20 years and had not walked in her "single mom" shoes. By the end of the book, tears were streaming down my face, as I could relate to so many circumstances that she touched upon and found myself highlighting things applicable to me, my husband, my 15 year old son and my 19 year old daughter. "To Love and be Cherished" is a true testament to "never judge a book by its cover" (literally) as I related to the content in its entirety although I have a completely different set of circumstances. Amazing! Religious or not, and single or not, male or female, it illustrates the importance of strong core values and it guides you to conviction of respecting one's self; those core values apply not only to the attentive single woman reader but also to the attentive male reader that would want to emulate those actions of a respectful, perfect partner.
-Laney Cavazos, Mom and Happily Married

Kirsten is an amazing writer! I am doing some soul searching and a lot of crying as I read. It has opened my eyes about being a better person. I can be a better partner from this awakening. I will do better and it's your book that helped me see that! I hope that it will continue to open my eyes about myself so I can love and cherish as well as being cherished and loved!
-Melynda Wendell, Widowed Single Mom

"To Love and Be Cherished" is a must read for any woman, no matter what relationship stage you find yourself in. Kirsten offers true principles in a real and honest way that made me feel like she was having a conversation with me as a friend. Though I am already married, I was able to take away from the book and apply it in areas in my own relationship that has helped strengthen my marriage.
-Chelsea Rumohr, Former Single Mom Now Happily Married

Every single girl/woman should read this book. I am so thankful for you Kirsten, you are the single most influential woman in my life. You are a wonderful mentor, sister and friend to so many women. Your heart is so genuine and I loved seeing your story in print. You inspire me to be better than I am today. I loved your book! I could hear your voice the entire way through. I wish I had these tools much earlier in life but am soooo thankful that I had the opportunity to be one of your first readers. I can't wait to share this gift with my nieces and friends, girls need to know this, they need to know their worth. Dating is so hard these days and compromising values and standards are pretty normal. Thank you for sharing your story.

-Angela Purchase, Single Mom to an Awesome Son

Kirsten, you nailed it out of the park! I learned so much. This book has changed me! There are so many things I want to quote in my planner for daily reading! I will definitely be sharing with my 16 year old daughter. The book addresses so many issues that many women face. It's deep yet light, very attainable and easy to read. I can see the content turned in to a great class for teens or adults.   I can't wait to share with my friends! Great job! Xo

-Kelly Wilson, Married Mom of 2 Teens

This book has opened my mind and heart so much, to not only the mistakes I was making in dating but in other relationships as well! It is truly a godsend, wonderfully written, and so easy to apply to my life.

-Andi Childers, Single Mom

All I can say, Kirsten, is that this is a wonderful way for women to grow and value themselves. Having been friends with you since middle school, I have known some, but not all of your challenges and triumphs. I am so proud of you for sharing your story - it's not easy to bare your heart to the world. Even as a woman who has been happily married for almost 25 years, I learned things that could help me improve my relationship. So proud of you and I plan to encourage both of my daughters to read and think about your book - even though they are both in committed relationships, they are young and still learning. Love you, friend!

-Stephanie Romagnoli, Happily Married, Grandma, Mom of 2 Adult Daughters

Often we allow our past to dictate our lives. Through her own challenges, Kirsten Ross gives us a voice on how to change patterns in our lives and become the person God wants us to be. This book will inspire all who read it!

-Linda Mashni, Mom and Grandmother

I wish that I had this book as a single woman to navigate the complexities of dating. You don't always view dating as complex but it certainly is as you read through the areas that Kirsten has profoundly identified. The principles outlined here are valid and have helped remind myself that I am not the only one who was desperately searching for love for years in all the wrong places. As a Christian woman, I am thankful to have this book as a reminder for myself in my married life as well as a resource to pass on to my single friends. I can't thank Kirsten enough for sharing her wisdom with the rest of us.

-Tiffany Woodward, Former Single Mom now Happily Married

This book is going to change the lives of so many... everyone needs to read it! Kirsten Ross Vogel, you have done an amazing job putting into words what we need to hear. Being single in today's society, with so many being raised by single parents, has it's challenges. But, those that have your book, as a tool to guide them, have a chance at a brighter future. Your person journey is inspiring and I am blessed to call you my friend. I cannot wait to be able to share this with everyone I know... so they can do the same. This is what you call making an impact on the world...

-Shawn Suarez Downie, Former Single Mom, Wife and Nana

Kirsten, this book is going to change lives. It will challenge those folks that need it. It will motivate them to look into themselves first before falling for someone just to have someone in their lives. Within the first few pages, I was already creating a mental note of who I know that needs to read it. Parents need to share this with their children, girls and boys. Every age group can benefit from your story. I have been with my husband and best friend for over 28 years. We will be celebrating our 25th anniversary in May. By no stretch of the imagination has it been anywhere near perfect, but our love has survived all of our trials and continues to grow on this incredible journey together. I learned a few things and was reminded of others. It was easy to stay focused. You give great, realistic & attainable life goals for securing happiness with someone extra special. Having a God base in your life helps tremendously. Thank you for giving me the opportunity to share in your adventure.

-Dawn Evennou, Your friend, supporter and happily married mom

To Love
And Be Cherished

THE ULTIMATE GUIDE TO FINDING
TRUE LOVE WITH A REAL MAN

Kirsten E. Vogel

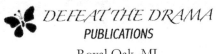

DEFEAT THE DRAMA
PUBLICATIONS
Royal Oak, MI

TO LOVE AND BE CHERISHED:
The Ultimate Guide to Finding True Love with a Real Man

All Rights Reserved ©Defeat the Drama Publishing 2016

Defeat the Drama™ is a Registered Trademark

This book is intended as a reference volume only, not as a medical or mental health manual. The author is not licensed as an educational consultant, teacher, psychologist, counselor, psychiatrist, or medical professional. In the case of a need for any such expertise consult with the appropriate professional. This book has not been created to be specific to any individual's situation or needs. This book details the author's personal experiences with and opinions about relationships. Recollections of events and opinions about what experiences meant are based on the author's own recall, perceptions and interpretations of those experiences.

Every effort has been made to make this book as accurate as possible. However, there may be typographical and or content errors and outdated. Information in this book is intended only to educate and entertain. The author and publisher shall have no liability or responsibility to any person or entity regarding any loss or damage incurred, or alleged to have incurred, directly or indirectly, by the information contained in this book. You hereby agree to be bound by this disclaimer or you may return this book within the guarantee time period for a full refund (thirty days).

This book may not be reproduced, transmitted, or stored in whole or in part by any means, including graphic, electronic, or mechanical without the express written consent of the publisher except in the case of brief quotations embodied in critical articles and reviews.

ISBN 978-0-692-64531-4

Editor Margaret O'Donnell, Book Sense

PRINTED IN THE UNITED STATES OF AMERICA

You are here for a purpose. There may be fears, self-doubt,

anger, uncertainty, and diminished self-esteem

standing in the way for you right now, but there is hope

— for you and for your future.

Be strong, bold, and courageous, whatever that means for you.

Focus on the part of you that knows without doubt that

you were perfectly and wonderfully made.

It might be buried deep, but find it and hold on.

That is truth, regardless of what you have been told.

And always remember — you are valuable and worthy of great love!

~ Kirsten

To Love And Be Cherished

THE ULTIMATE GUIDE TO FINDING
TRUE LOVE WITH A REAL MAN

Table Of Contents

A True Love Story... The Start

You, like many single women, yearn for that one *True Love*. The man who will sweep you off your feet, stand by your side, and help you feel loved and cherished for a lifetime. Whether you're a seasoned dater or a teen just getting started, if your goal is *True Love*, I have written this book for you.

See, I have been where you are. I have been a young single person in the dating scene, a wife, mother, a dating single mom and now a partner in a *True Love* relationship with a *Real Man*. I have felt disappointment, frustration, anger and resignation. I have feared that the vision I had for my love would never become real. I did not take a straight path to *True Love*, by any means, but I have arrived there. I can certainly say, without hesitation, that I feel like one of the luckiest women in the world! I am married to a wonderful man named Eric. He is supportive, caring, compassionate, a great listener and a wonderful role model for our two growing boys. I am cherished and loved. We live a God centered life.

I have gained knowledge through my own life experiences. In addition, I can share what I've learned over the course of more than ten years working with hundreds of individuals dealing with relationship challenges. I am a Leadership and Family Business Coach. On the surface it sounds like I might only help with work struggles. However, the breadth of my work extends far beyond the professional realm. Family businesses can be fraught with complex personal relationships. And, as I say to each new client, "You are who you are in both your life and in your work. Working on one area will impact both." This invites sharing of not jut work issues but also of struggles in significant personal relationships. As a result, I have had the privilege of helping many clients transform both married and dating relationships. In addition, I have compassion for single moms, as I was one for eight years, and have helped many navigate the difficulties of their dating lives.

This book is a culmination of lessons I've learned from my own life experiences, real life stories as illustrations, strategies I've gained through supporting others through their relationship challenges and time-tested words of wisdom from the Bible. I will provide some recommendations in this book to help you transform your reading into action but there is also a *Companion Workbook* available that will help you dive deeper into the material. You can find it by visiting ToLoveAndBeCherished.com/Products. I encourage you to move through it as you read the book to take your aha moments into action. I want everyone who longs for *True Love* to have what I have!

Throughout this book I will share stories from my personal relationships with you, but for now let me start in the middle, with Eric's proposal. I think it speaks volumes about who he is and will give you a window into our relationship. We originally met each other at our church, Kensington Community Church in Michigan, and when he decided to propose to me after two years of courtship he fittingly arranged for his proposal to take place there. It was a very snowy night as we headed out for dinner. He mentioned, "I need to drop a book off to Alex at the church. We'll swing by there on our way." Saturday night service was in full swing when we arrived, but he walked me into the side chapel, a smaller, more intimate space. The altar was covered with beautifully glowing white candles. They lit the space and gave warmth to the room. He held my hand, guided me up the steps and knelt in front of me. He gazed into my eyes and spoke about how we met, how much he loved me and how excited he was for God's plans for our lives to unfold.

It was perfection.

We left for what I thought would be a quiet dinner to celebrate. He said we had reservations at an Italian restaurant nearby.

What I didn't know was that a room full of friends and

family members were waiting for me there. When I walked in I was overwhelmed with emotion. I had never had a surprise party before!

I exclaimed, "Wow, and I thought that getting engaged was my only surprise tonight!"

The response I got was not what I expected, as they all cried out in excitement, "You got engaged?!"

"Aren't you here to celebrate our engagement?" I asked.

"No! We're here to celebrate you!"

I soon learned that Eric had sent an invitation explaining that I'd never had a surprise party and that all who were receiving it meant the world to me. It said, "I want her to know how much she means to you. Join in a celebration of Kirsten."

Eric turned to me and explained, "From now on, if you are ever feeling lonely, I want you to remember tonight and know that you are loved. Everyone is here tonight because they love you and want to celebrate *you*."

It made the night even more significant. They weren't there to celebrate an event with us they were there to celebrate me. I was overwhelmed and humbled. He had put much care and planning into the engagement to make it so very special.

Since our wedding we have been truly blessed. Have there been difficult times? Of course. But we are living in a true partnership that helps us navigate life's challenges. Eric enjoyed a seamless transition into step- fatherhood, not a frequent occurrence in modern families, especially with boys the ages of ours, who were both in middle school at the time. We have a lot of laughter and love in our home. We enjoy great communication. We are each other's biggest fans. I feel confident being myself. I believe that it is the strong foundation we created by using the dating strategies I will share in this book that have afforded us the opportunity to create the relationship and life we have today.

People sometimes look at my life and the positive approach I live by and believe that I've always had it easy. And that's just not true. I have actually had my fair share of challenges. I have gotten to where I am through blood, sweat and a whole lot of tears, and, of course, with the love of God and His favor. He was absolutely with us every step of the way. I was a single mom for eight years before marrying Eric and one of the gifts I got from that single mom time, was a closer relationship to God and my growing faith.

I feel that it's important that I share some of my struggles and triumphs in this book, not to say, "Woe is me." But people might have a tendency to think, "I could never have that. She's different." And the truth is, I'm not. We are all broken and as a broken, imperfect person who has made many mistakes I was able to find *True Love*. I want you to know that you *can* have what I have.

I've done plenty of things, shall we say, less than optimally, over many years of dating and more relationships than I care to think about. I try to avoid the word "wrong." Life is all about learning and we can make mistakes, learn some important lessons from them, grow and move on. So, "wrong" just feels a bit too negative.

I have used physical intimacy as a form of validation, and dated when I really needed to focus on my own healing. Before Eric, I've definitely picked the wrong kind of men many times. I've led with my physical appearance rather than my heart, kept silly things on my list of "must-haves" when in the scheme of life they weren't really important. In my twenties I had "Must be a good dancer" at the top of my list. I later realized that dancing is a nice bonus, but not a make-or- break trait.

And I've experienced verbal abuse. Abuse is something no one wants to admit is part of his or her life. To learn to recognize abuse, remove myself and heal was exceptionally difficult but were some of the first steps towards acquiring *True Love*. Abuse has torn down my confidence and self-assurance until I no longer even recognized myself. The loving voice in my head was drowned out and my mind became consumed with self-blame, unmet expectations, and feelings of failure. I could no longer feel my intuition, let alone follow it. My entire life became focused on earning love and acceptance.

The more failure I felt, the deeper I sank into an emotional black hole. The voice in my heart that used to sing out, "You are wonderfully and perfectly made," grew quieter, and quieter, until I could no longer hear it. The words "you are good enough and worthy" became nothing but a whisper. I was beaten down, broken, low on self-esteem and self-worth.

I was motivated to learn new strategies for creating a

healthy relationship. In many instances, I had not chosen well or in accordance with God's design for a partnership. I made a pledge to do better and I will share my strategies here.

My hope is that, in following this guide to True Love, you will find comfort and courage in the parts of my story I share and an understanding of the steps you can take. I pray that, as you read this book, the voice in your own heart grows louder and you find yourself stronger, encouraged, empowered and more intentional about your dating. And I want you to believe to your core that you are valuable, loveable, loved and cherished now. With or without a man you are whole and have enough.

And, while this book is not specifically for single moms, I am going to include some of what I call "Single Mom Moments." I've dated both as a single and as a single mom. There is a difference.

Here is the first one.

Single Mom Moment: Loneliness

I, like many other single moms, landed in the role doubting myself and feeling ill-equipped. It was not a role I would have chosen for myself had it not been necessary. I had to work to embrace it.

When I was a single mom, from the outside looking in, people might have thought that my life was great. I had two great boys, a house, a business -- so much to be grateful for!

Gratitude was where I spent a good portion of my time even then. But it took work sometimes. Outsiders likely didn't see the fear, the overwhelm, the anxiety, the feeling less than, the loneliness, the clawing my way back from the devastation I felt from the failure. They couldn't know about the effort of just stepping back up into, "I am okay. I have value. I am a good person."

I missed the days of working side by side with a partner, planning an agenda, accomplishing daily tasks together, sharing the responsibilities of running a house and caring for kids. I yearned to have it again, especially on the days when the weight of responsibilities felt too hard to bear alone; on those days when I had to take slow, deep breaths and focus on one task at a time; when things went wrong or I was pushed out of my comfort zone, dealing, yet again, with a task that I knew nothing about and had no idea how to accomplish.

My boys wanted partnership for me too. They were so young, and yet almost immediately began asking, "Mom, are you going to get married again?" "Why do you ask?" I queried. "We just want you to have someone who really loves you." Pure sweetness and very aligned with my own heart's desire.

When you get divorced or end any significant relationship you don't just start a new life chapter you begin a new book. You close the cover on one section of your life to begin anew. The outline you created for your life's future must be shredded but it's hard to let go of the vision and move on. There's hurt and anger to maneuver and release. You no longer share that history with anyone. Pictures lose their meaning. A memory jar needs to be purged so that you can begin anew. People leave your life. Pieces of your family are no more. Some people in your life will never understand.

I knew that being a single mom would be hard. It was one of the things that kept me in a marriage for as I long as I stayed. I knew that holidays would be rough. I knew that I would have to endure periods of time away from my boys, something that I hadn't previously experienced with my hands-on approach to motherhood. I knew that all responsibilities would fall on me, though I didn't have the full sense of what that weight would feel like, the all-encompassing immensity of it. I was as prepared as I could be.

The one thing that I did not anticipate at all, however, was the loneliness. My life had always been so full of people. I had lots of friends and many family-centered activities to enjoy with them.

We had fall barbeques with neighbors every year and a get-together for the boys' birthdays, a huge gathering with friends and family for Christmas, a Super Bowl party next door, a great family friendly New Year's Eve party just down the road.

When I became a single mom it all stopped. Well, the neighborhood barbeque still happens. We've just never been invited again. And I know the Super Bowl party happened at least a few more times; I was just no longer a guest.

I was still fully family-oriented, so I assumed that those relationships would all continue. But when, suddenly, I didn't have a spouse, I no longer fit into that world.

I wasn't ready to design a life around singledom, though, to start using babysitters so I could head out on the town. I was determined that my boys would continue to be a part of my social life, whatever that would look like. When the kids went to bed at night it was just me. Holidays came around and I had invitations for those gatherings but it would never feel the same as family.

Human beings have an innate desire to be in relationship, to share the smiles and knowing looks of appreciation when your kids do something cute, absurd, or funny. I was no exception. I was lonely!

I had entered into my previous marriage with as much hope and commitment as any bride. The plans I had, the outline I created did not work out. I had not chosen well, and it was not a God-centered marriage, which I later learned was a key ingredient to achieving the relationship I desired.

I still believed with all of my heart that we are meant to live lives filled with joy and that our key relationship should be one of intimacy, where it is safe to be vulnerable, where we are challenged to reach our full potential through continual growth. I vowed to have that, and now I Do.

You don't have to be a Christian or even believe in God to enjoy and learn from this book. I will talk about Him, though. And I will reference the Bible. The strategies I will share are not the only ones. They aren't perfect, but they do include a relationship with God, and have helped Eric and me to create a great marriage. It is my belief that my faith and God's direction had a huge impact on my healing and transformation, and my ability to find *True Love*.

I believe wholeheartedly that creating and maintaining the best kind of relationship with your partner in life requires God in the center. Humans are self-centered by nature. Just spend time with any toddler and you'll see. Their favorite word is almost always "mine!" Sharing is not innate, it is learned, and I don't believe that core selfishness ever fully leaves us, but just gets tucked away. We learn to have an outward focus, empathy, concern for others. But deep down inside, if we are truthful, is that little toddler still screaming, "Mine!" I have a favorite blanket. If someone else in this house is using it, I immediately feel the call within: "Mine!" Thankfully, I have mastered the art of keeping the sentiment to myself but, I can't deny it is there.

What I learned, and why God matters, is that designing a truly loving partnership doesn't happen if you focus only on your own needs. God helps us be more selfless and to place our focus where it should be. God also removes some of the burden of looking to each other for fulfillment. If we allow it, He will fill us and give us guidance. I do not proclaim this to be the only path to a wonderful marriage. I do believe that it is a great way.

You may feel differently about God's place in your pursuit of *True Love*. You can still learn from my experience. I will make a request, however. The same one that I make with all clients and mentees I work with around any new concept. When you feel defensive or irritated by an idea or strategy that I share, whether about God or anything else, I ask that you just . . . *try it on for size.* Give it a whirl to see if it works. What have you got to lose by looking at the issue, challenge or circumstance from a new perspective? You never know the positive difference it might make.

During more than ten years of coaching I have been witness to the stay-stuck strategies our brains can create when we are adverse to change. We can justify, explain away, and refuse to even consider the possibility of a new truth. More often than not, after breaking through the wall of defense, people reap the rewards of the transformation initiated by a simple shift in perspective.

. . . try it on for size.

Remember, trying a new perspective or strategy doesn't mean you *have* to adopt it. It doesn't require you to let go of current beliefs or habits. Later I will be making the distinction between trying and committing. Giving it a whirl isn't a commitment for life. It's just a commitment to test or consider a new idea or perspective in the moment with an open heart and mind.

Where you start thinking, "that makes no sense," or "heck no," I ask you to just take a few breaths and push through those immediate negative thoughts to consider, "what if . . ."

If you are one of those people who gets turned off by "God Talk" I encourage you to push through your feelings and read on. I promise, there will be no pressure to change your beliefs and plenty of ways to benefit from the information here regardless. But the Bible provides some time-tested wisdom, which can be applied to modern, real life situations, as you will see.

For instance, I am going to talk about purity in dating. Yep, and I'll use that old fashioned word too. *BUT*, I'm going to give you some motivation beyond just "the Bible says." See, the thing is, the Bible isn't really a book of limiting rules. We limit ourselves with the addictions, fears or false beliefs that chain us down and make our lives smaller. The Bible shows us how to cast off the chains. Take just a moment to think about where you've failed to achieve your goals. Was it because you couldn't muster the self-discipline? Maybe some bad choices made it impossible or a fear of failure caused you to quit. Much of what limits us comes from within, and is in stark contrast to what God designs for us.

God loved us so much that He gave us free will. He doesn't make us follow Him or His rules. He just wants us to because He wants the best for us. His guidelines, shared with us years ago, can save us from a lot of heartache, all that stuff we do to ourselves in life and in dating.

So, I will share some of His guidelines in a way that will make them practical for you in today's world. And, you'll still get to choose what you do. No judgment here!

CARE *Groups*

📖 *"And let us consider how to stir up one another to love and good works, not neglecting to meet together, as is the habit of some, but encouraging one another, and all the more as you see the Day drawing near."* (Hebrews 10:24-25)

I encourage you to move through this book with a group of single women. You'll be able to share ideas, celebrate successes, cry over missteps and hold each other accountable. It is also a great way to bond!

Life is meant to be lived in community. Why not take this challenge with other women working towards a similar goal? You can call your gatherings a "Party with a Purpose." Your search for True Love will be more successful if guided by the strategies you will find here and shared with a group of women already in your life or who you will join together for support. I call them CARE groups because these women will become your

Cheerleaders

Accountability Partners

Reality Checkers

Encouragers

Let's look at each individually:

Cheerleaders: Your CARE group members will cheer you up and cheer you on as you enter and navigate the dating scene. And while it will arm you with strategies to avoid some of its pitfalls, or at least to identify them more quickly than you have in the past, there is no guarantee that this journey will happen without frustration or strife. It will be helpful to have a team in your corner providing the positive reinforcement to keep you working towards your dream.

Accountability Partners: Chances are quite good that the strategies in this guide are different from the way you've operated in your dating life in the past. Some of what I'll ask you to do will seem counter-intuitive. You will be asked to delay gratification, set healthy boundaries and take note of red flags that you may have ignored in the past. Decisions, actions, thought processes may all be different from what you are used to. It is great to have a team to help you stay committed as you work on new habits. A team of people who can share the truth of what they see and help you focus on behaving in new ways in your dating practices, a team you can trust and be vulnerable with, who will lovingly help you stay committed to what may initially feel very foreign and uncomfortable.

Reality Checkers: Without even realizing it, you may be in the habit of overlooking red flags or indications that a potential partner may not have the right intentions. Too often we want to believe the best of others, and then miss the warning signs that should send us running. Your CARE Group members can provide objective observation. They can nicely point out what you may be blind to or are unwilling to acknowledge.

Encouragers: The dating world can be rough. Anytime you operate in this realm, you are opening yourself up to rejection. Your CARE group can be there to remind you of your value and help you to see what you are better off knowing now rather than later. The end of a bad relationship is a gift, really. Better to receive the blessing of the end than to be dragged on despite the poor fit. Your team can remind you that ending something that was doomed leaves you open and available for your Real Man. They will also continue to remind you that you are wonderfully and beautifully made, valued, loved and lovable.

CARE Group Guidelines

Do you already have a community of single women? This will give you the excuse to get together more regularly. You will cement your relationships while you move towards your goals. Don't have a community? What a great reason to find or create one! Check with others where you work, reconnect with old friends, post a note on Facebook, start a group through your church, or use Meetup.com. There are many ways to find other women to join your mission.

When you do begin to meet use the Companion Workbook to guide your time together and establish some ground rules for making your group successful. Create a judgment free zone. Women can share their experiences and lessons learned, but should not be controlling or dictate the actions of others. We all have our own pace and not everyone will be equally ready to make necessary changes. Give each other grace. Make your group a respectful, comfortable place to share and encourage one another. Take turns sharing. No aggression, no jealousy or competition, no subgroups or gossip. Keep information that is shared among you confidential. Empathize, don't criticize.

> 📖 *Two are better than one, because they have a good reward for their toil. For if they fall, one will lift up his fellow. But woe to him who is alone when he falls and has not another to lift him up! (Ecclesiastes 4:9-11)*

Now, let's move forward to the first step. Making your plan.

Plan

📖 *For I know the plans I have for you," declares the LORD, "plans to prosper you and not to harm you, plans to give you hope and a future." (Jeremiah 29:11)*

If you don't know where you're heading you will probably end up lost. I feel I've ended up in the wrong place many times in my dating life. It's time to get specific about what your *Real Man* looks like and what *True Love* means to you.

A few years ago I had the opportunity to hear Beth Moore speak. She's a popular author, Bible teacher, and founder of Living Proof Ministries, a Bible-based organization for women based in Houston, Texas. For several hours, she taught on the concept of, "your heart's desire." According to her, God puts a desire on our hearts. It's a message that prompts us to know His vision for our life. For our purposes we'll focus on the specific desires of your heart when it comes to your significant relationship.

According to Ms. Moore, the desire of your heart will stand the test of time and circumstance.

So many women who try to find True Love have had missteps that are so discouraging they just store the desire away. Being unable to see a clear path to your goal can make it too painful to pursue.

Now is the time to dive deep inside yourself and listen for that desire. What do you really want? What if you could have it?

You don't want to experience the desire as a generic feeling. Take the time to document specifically what you want in your significant relationship.

In this section you are going to get clear about what you seek. What is your desire? What would True Love look like and what qualities must a Real Man have for you?

Let's start by defining some of the terms used in the subtitle of the book. We each have our own vision of who our perfect Real Man is, so these are just my conceptual definitions, which you can apply to your own specific criteria as a starting point.

Real Man:

I think the concept of a Real Man lives in our hearts as women almost from the start. But it's something we seldom actually define or put into words. Perhaps this is why we miss the mark so often in our dating. Without a specific target we fall for something short of what we really long for.

Some elements of the "Real Man" definition will be specific to you. However, I believe there are some that will be common to most.

While I was an active dater I slowly built a list of the qualities that were important in a partner and in a relationship, as many people do. Dating can be a great learning experience as you meander your way through all kinds of personality types and character traits. You become more and more adept at weeding out bad relationship candidates. Here is part of what I concluded.

A Real Man will be kind, polite, respectful and patient. He won't play games or keep you guessing. He'll let you know where you stand and how he feels with both his words and actions. He'll have integrity, which means those words and actions match. He will seek to protect all of you; your mind, heart, spirit, soul and body. His goal will be partnership, never manipulation or control. He will listen without defensiveness and seek to fully understand. He will lift you up not tear you down.

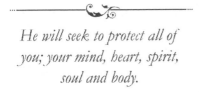

He will seek to protect all of you; your mind, heart, spirit, soul and body.

A Real Man will give you grace without being a pushover. The perfect blend of loving all of who you are with the ability to kindly and gently call you on your stuff.

A Real Man does not display over the top masculinity. He will be strong and confident but not overpowering. A competitive spirit is good and will drive him to succeed. He will not be an egomaniac who can't bear to lose. He embodies the perfect blend between cocky and confident. A focus on serving others over getting his own needs met. He'll have a heart of gold and a love for God.

If we get to the center of our desires, I believe that we all want to feel cared for. Not owned or dominated. But we want to feel that a man is a strength beside us and will protect us, whether it's physically or financially. We want to feel cherished. This is beyond feeling loved. We want him to delight in us.

The reality is that few, if any, of us moves through life without picking up some baggage. None of us is perfect. So, to expect a "Real Man" to be perfect is too much. However, a Real Man will have some understanding of his shortcomings, a self-awareness and willingness to explore where he can improve. To say it more succinctly, he owns his junk.

Single Mom Moment: How Will He Be as a Stepdad?

In the world of single mom-hood a requirement for a Real Man is that he see himself as a full partner with you when it comes to your kids. Can he put aside ill feelings with the kids' dad? Can he step in with grace knowing that he may play a leading role in the logistics of life while taking a back seat in the official role? He must be willing to step in to the work of the role without the guarantee of any acknowledgement. The dad will likely continue in the main role as dad regardless of the time, money, or energy he invests in your kids. Stepdad is a tough role that requires stamina, heart, grace, restraint, passion and selflessness. Stepping into the work of daily duties without the starring title for the big events. If he is not able to accept the role fully, not willing to stand by your side through the day-to-day

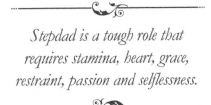

Stepdad is a tough role that requires stamina, heart, grace, restraint, passion and selflessness.

responsibilities of parenthood, he isn't a man suited for a single mom. If you carry most of the burden, then you end up living different lives and it becomes difficult to avoid resentment, a definite relationship-buster.

True Love

There is a song that I feel illustrates true, long-lasting love. I urge you to find and listen to the song "He Was Walking Her Home" by Mark Schultz. He is a popular Contemporary Christian Artist. The song is from his album "Broken and Beautiful Expanded Version" and was released in 2006. I think it captures the essence of what we yearn for in our significant love relationship. I remember vividly the experience I had the first time I heard it. My kids were in elementary school at the time and I sat in the parking lot waiting for the bell to ring. I was a tired, overwhelmed single mom still fueled by the hope of finding a great relationship. A friend had given me Mark's CD as a gift and, as was my practice, I queued up each song quickly, listening to the beginning of each to get a feel for the CD's offerings. The expanded version of the song begins with a spoken narration from Mark about how his elderly neighbors were the inspiration for his writing. It was a sweet story and I found myself slowing to listen to the full song. Here are just a few words from it:

Looking back

He sees it all

It was her first date the night he came to call

. . . .

[Chorus:]

He was walking her home

And holding her hand

Oh the way she smiled it stole the breath right out of him

Down that old road

With the stars up above

He remembers where he was the night he fell in love

He was walking her home

. . . .

He walked her through the best days of her life

Sixty years together and he never left her side

As the words and melody of the song painted the story, something stirred deep in my soul. It brought up the pain of lost possibilities, the disappointment in futures unrealized, and a deep, deep yearning. My heart and soul knew that this was the kind of love I wanted to experience. While already more mature than the young lovers described in the story, a flicker of hope that I could still find that True Love flamed in me and ignited the longing for it with a fury. Tears began to stream down my face and I held my breath so that the parents in the cars surrounding me would not hear my sobs.

Would I find my special forever-someone in time to create a lifetime of memories together?

We often talk about love as a feeling and it certainly begins with a zing. True and sustainable love, however, is a choice and requires action. Each partner in the relationship must commit to patience, humility, respect and service.

True Love means trusting one another enough to be vulnerable to share your insecurities, weaknesses and brokenness and know that you'll be accepted, safe, and loved. It's a deep understanding of each other.

It's being together for years and still smiling when you arrive to find them home. It's a warm embrace that gives comfort in a moment. It's security, and commitment, and a passion for seeing each other succeed.

It's thinking of one another. Communicating with nothing more than an expression because you know each other so well.

True Love is respect, playfulness and kindness.

I love that my husband serves me, and when I say thank you his response, almost without fail is, "My pleasure." I believe that it is God's presence in our marriage that makes this possible.

📖 *God is love. Whoever lives in love lives in God, and God in them. [17] ... [18] There is no fear in love. But perfect love drives out fear, because fear has to do with punishment. The one who fears is not made perfect in love. [19] We love because he first loved us. (1 John 4:17-19)*

In the Bible and quotes below God shares a vision of love in marriage and asks husbands to be not only leaders but Servant Leaders in their homes and to love their wives as Christ loved the church. If you study this a bit you will find that Christ loved the church a lot! As a matter of fact, as a servant leader, He put the church above His own wants, needs and desires. According to the Bible, in a marriage it is a husband's duty to do the same for his family and he is to help his wife to fulfill her purpose and destiny. It is a wife's duty is to respect her husband.

Here are a few verses that summarize God's design of love and marriage:

📖 *[4] Love is patient, love is kind. It does not envy, it does not boast, it is not proud. [5] It does not dishonor others, it is not self-seeking, it is not easily angered, it keeps no record of wrongs. [6] Love does not delight in evil but rejoices with the truth. [7] It always protects, always trusts, always hopes, always perseveres. [8] Love never fails. (1 Corinthians 13:4-8)*

📖 *[25] Husbands, love your wives, just as Christ loved the church and gave himself up for her. (Ephesians 5:2)*

📖 *Husbands, love your wives, and do not be harsh with them. (Colossians 3:19)*

📖 *³³ However, each one of you also must love his wife as he loves himself, and the wife must respect her husband. (Ephesians 5:33)*

📖 *A servant-leader does not lord over others. Instead he... serves others selflessly. (Matthew 20:26-28)*

📖 *In everything that he does, a servant-leader is motivated by... love for God and love for his family and neighbors. (1 John 4:7)*

So, the Bible asks a husband to serve his wife with love, help her live out her purpose and put his own needs aside for those of his family. True Love requires selflessness from both and a partnership that leaves each working together to love, respect and cherish.

Create Your Vision

I assume that since you are reading this book, you are seeking to find your forever-someone. This guide is not about finding "a" relationship, a warm body or friend-with-benefits, the goal is about finding "the" relationship. You may have resigned yourself to the fact that you will never find *True Love*. That desire for that relationship may be tucked away under years of failed attempts, disappointments, hurts, fears and feelings of not good enough. But the aspiration is still there.

Your first step is to release the vision you carry for your True Love relationship from underneath the layers of hurt and disappointment. Your heart knows what you yearn for in your forever-someone. If you had your heart's desire what would it be? Who would he be? How would he treat you? How would you spend your time together? How would you communicate? How would he help with your kids? What kind of role model would he be for them? What kind of personality does he have? What are his dreams and pursuits?

Think big, dig deep and begin to brainstorm a list, not of nice-to-haves but of your ultimate wishes from your heart. Not what society says you should want, not what your friends think you should have, but what your heart desires for you. Know what you want so you can evaluate future relationships objectively. It won't necessarily conform to what the current man in your life wants. Your list will become your guidepost.

I created the list below to describe the relationship I desired, both as an independent woman and as a single mom. I had a separate list that included more detail about the kind of man I wanted. I won't share that. It's hard enough to listen to your own heart when there is so much noise from the world.

My list can serve as a starting point for yours, but of course make the list you create specific to your desires.

This next section is exactly what I wrote years ago. It is the unedited version from the document I created. And, I am so happy to report that I have SHRLP! And I want everyone to have what I have.

Kirsten's Vision

S upportive

H ealthy

L oving

R espectful

P artnership

- ❖ Creating a life
- ❖ Making things happen
- ❖ Supporting each other's passions
- ❖ Lifting each other up
- ❖ Working together through the good and the muck
- ❖ Fully integrated
- ❖ Give and take
- ❖ Playfulness
- ❖ Sharing
- ❖ Modeling great partnership to the next generation
- ❖ Connecting at a deep level
- ❖ Growing
- ❖ Learning
- ❖ Motivating
- ❖ Energizing
- ❖ Using our lives, talents and time together
- ❖ Cherishing
- ❖ Emotional safety
- ❖ Warmth
- ❖ Acceptance
- ❖ Connection
- ❖ Passion

I can feel it! I can see it!!!

So often when people first meet they learn that they are compatible at dinner, can go to the same movies, can hold a conversation in the car. But what are they talking about? Politics, work, what happened that day, a new television show...

Other times people cover the big topics; values, commitments, passions, visions for the future, feelings, injuries, and weaknesses.

Sharing, accepting and committing to the core are the most important things. The rest just feels like logistics.

- ❖ It feels like if you respect each other and

- ❖ Know the weaknesses and treat them with tenderness and

- ❖ Know the desires and passions and honor them and

- ❖ Make a commitment to do this for each other and

- ❖ Make a commitment to continue growing and learning as individuals and

- ❖ Make a commitment to always be open and honest and

- ❖ Make a commitment to own your own junk

- ❖ Together you work to negotiate around the other stuff - the logistics of life.

These are the keys to SHLRP

I recommend you create something similar for yourself. Following are a few steps to follow that will help you gain clarity and document your vision.

As you create your list try to think of the qualities of the person you are looking for, rather than the activities that interest them. Activities can change as life priorities and physical abilities transition.

What does your heart desire? What qualities or characteristics do you want in your *Real Man*? Use the list as a guide not a rulebook. How do you want love to feel?

You'll find additional steps and things to think about in the *Companion Workbook*.

Core Values

I recommend that you get clear about your core values. These are guiding principles that can drive your decisions, whether you are aware or not. You will want to find someone who shares at least some of your core values, and who embodies them. For instance, if one of your core values is integrity you will not pair well with a man who uses white lies, even innocently.

Here is a list of core values. It is not comprehensive or in any particular order. It will help you get the creative juices flowing. Share with your CARE Group too. Maybe they've seen some things in you that you aren't aware of.

Core Values List

Humor	Partnership	Productivity
Directness	Service	Contribution
Excellence	Free Spirit	Focus
Romance	Recognition	Harmony
Accomplishment	Orderliness	Goal Oriented
Honesty	Success	Accuracy
Adventure	Lack of Pretense	Zest
Tradition	To Be Known	Growth
Aesthetics	Participation	Performance
Collaboration	Community	Personal Power
Freedom to Choose	Connectedness	Acknowledgement
Comradeship	Lightness	Spirituality
Empowerment	Full Self-Expression	Integrity
Creativity	Independence	Nurturing
Joy	Beauty	Authenticity
Risk Taking	Peaceful	Elegance
Vitality	Trust	Wholeness
Truth	Freedom	Charity
Inner Peace	Faith	Equality
Nobility	Humility	Kindness

Love	Safety	Self-Worth
Positive Attitude	Justice	Humility
Love		Dignity
Relationships	Community	Respect
Simplicity	Hope	Passion

I'm not promising a quick turnaround. If you are like I was, you have some preparation to do before you are ready for your forever-someone. You'll find more on that in the next chapter. Follow the steps in this book to help you remain positive, hopeful and prayerful. Stay connected with your CARE Group and you will get there. And know that you are beautiful, loved and wonderful today! Use your *Companion Workbook* to take your learning deeper.

Prepare

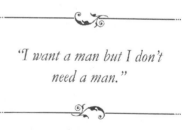

📖 *³ Your beauty should not come from outward adornment, such as elaborate hairstyles and the wearing of gold jewelry or fine clothes. ⁴ Rather, it should be that of your inner self, the unfading beauty of a gentle and quiet spirit, which is of great worth in God's sight. ⁵ (Peter 3:3-5)*

By now you should have done the work of defining what a *Real Man* is for you. You've written down the key characteristics and

"I want a man but I don't need a man."

behaviors he should exhibit, what his goals are, what is in his heart. You should have a sense of what your core values are. Now it is time to prepare yourself for the journey to *True Love.* Perhaps you've felt discouraged, frustrated, lonely or unlovable in this endeavor previously. This preparation step will help you enter into dating with a different frame of mind.

I want you to enter into dating with this as your driving belief: "I *want* a man but I don't *need* a man." Need means needy and you don't want that. Needy will have you attracting a different kind of man. Needy helps you tolerate what you shouldn't. Needy motivates you to transform yourself to meet his needs rather than suffer the loss of a relationship. The belief that having anyone is better than having no one is not truth, and you need to know that to your core. You are not looking for just *anyone* you are looking for "*the*" one. When you proceed from a place of strength, you will accept nothing less.

Have the courage to say no and the conviction to follow through if ending a relationship is required.

I want you to have the courage to say no and the conviction to follow through if ending a relationship is required.

It is risky to rely on dating for validation of your self-worth. You must already know your value. Know your strengths and weaknesses, give yourself grace and know you are fine no matter how it turns out. Your romantic relationship, or your lack of one, does not define you.

Defining your worth through dating leaves you vulnerable to settling, and too often the quest for a man becomes a competition. He's seen as a prize to win and other women are seen as something to conquer. You falsely believe that your value and self-esteem will soar if you can achieve this goal. In a pursuit of this nature, your focus shifts from where it should be, finding and developing your *True Love* relationship, to one resting solely on the conquest. You forget to notice who this man really is that you've dubbed a prize.

Recently I was listening to a radio program. A man had been caught cheating on his wife. They called him out on the air. He actually admitted it immediately, as if this would gain him points for honesty, though fessing up once caught isn't exactly the same as owning up. Was he embarrassed, remorseful or regretful? No, none of these emotions were expressed. His reaction was quite the opposite. In fact, he seemed boastful. It was obvious that, in his mind, his ability to drag two women along proved how awesome he was as a man. His moral compass was off. He had no remorse, no regret for the hurt he caused either woman, but rather took pride in the deception of each.

And yet, these two women began to fight for him on the air.

"He was with me last night! You need to step back!"

"I've been with him for 3 years. You need to walk away."

The focus for both women shifted to the competition. The man's perceived value increased proportionate to the size of the battle, and the self-worth of each became

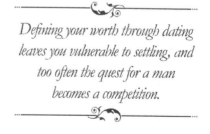

Defining your worth through dating leaves you vulnerable to settling, and too often the quest for a man becomes a competition.

wrapped up in the determination of who would win. Neither ego could handle a loss and neither woman stopped to think about what the win would really yield – a liar and a cheater for a mate.

This is the risk you run when you view the dating process as a measure of self-worth. You can end up tolerating more than you should. We are beautifully and wonderfully made but we don't know it. We think that rejection from a man seals our fate, or proves we are flawed, so we tolerate more than we should, hiding our own desires to become what we think he wants us to be. Avoiding the loss, and everything we fear it means, becomes more important than taking a stand for what we deserve.

Don't expect a relationship or another person to provide you with answers to the big questions about yourself. You must already know that the answers are yes:
Am I worthy?
Am I loveable?
Am I beautiful?
Am I good enough?
Am I okay?

The ultimate goal is to feel good in the knowledge of who you are and standing on solid self-esteem *before* you pursue a relationship. Then shift your focus here:
Is *he* worthy?
Is *he* loveable?
Is *he* good enough?
Is *he* beautiful on the inside?
Is *he* okay?
Should *I* reject *him*?

Always remember that you are already wonderful and valued. Whether you currently believe what the Bible says or not, this is truth. Regardless of your current circumstance, your history, your indiscretions, you are already loved and cherished. My hope is that you'll embrace this truth as part of your process of preparing.

What would it mean to know that God loves you right now? It would mean that you can enter into the dating world with a foundation of "I am already loved and cherished." I'm not asking you to commit to anything or change your current beliefs. All I ask is that you try it on for size for a bit. If it's a no that's okay too, just move forward with what you are comfortable.

📖 *"I have loved you with an everlasting love; I have drawn you with loving-kindness" (Jeremiah 31:3)*

📖 *The LORD your God is in your midst, a mighty one who will save; he will rejoice over you with gladness; he will quiet you by his love; he will exult over you with loud singing. (Zephaniah 3:17)*

If you have never done so, inviting God into your life requires nothing more than a simple prayer. "Dear God, I know that you sent Jesus to be my Savior, and that He died on the cross for my sins. Please forgive me of all of my sins, and come into my life and change me. In Jesus' Name, Amen."

📖 *⁹If you declare with your mouth, "Jesus is Lord," and believe in your heart that God raised him from the dead, you will be saved. (Romans 10:9)*

Your chances for a successful relationship are much better if you can enter it as a strong individual with a high sense of self-worth. Have a clear vision of the life you are trying to create, and an ability to communicate your feelings, wants and needs. You want True Love, not a dysfunctional or co-dependent relationship.

None of us moves through life without picking up some bad habits, hang ups, fears, and false beliefs that alter our behaviors or create relationship issues. It's not about avoiding the bad stuff, but what you do with it after it happens. It's just a part of life.

How often do you hear that the focus in dating is to be the best person? And I do agree that that is the start. Be your best self so that you can attract your best mate. Now, please don't read that as "be perfect." Perfection is an unachievable goal and self-improvement is a never-ending endeavor.

The goal can't be perfection, but honey, please don't be a hot mess!

People in relationships fit like pieces in a puzzle. What shape is your puzzle piece and what kind of person would you attract? From my observations I believe that people pleasers tend to end up with more aggressive types who want to be in control. I call them "people pushers." Commitment issues? You'll probably attract someone who loves doing the intimacy issues dance.

Your brokenness, unhealed, or your bad dating habits, left unchecked, may not allow you to feel attraction to the kind of man your heart desires. A healthy relationship might feel foreign and very uncomfortable. Does that strike a chord? Do you pick the same kind of man over and over to create the same relationship again and again?

It sounds so silly but I have to say this to my clients more often than you'd believe, "If you don't change, nothing changes."

So, get to a place where your heart only zings for the kind of man who will cherish you, to a place where you know to the depth of your core that you are worthy of *True Love*.

It's time to look at yourself and your life. Not to beat yourself up. No! That is a waste of energy. Give yourself grace. It is just time for a reality check. Are you at your best or do you have steps to get on your way?

Are you angry or bitter? Do you have abandonment issues? Are you a people pleaser who can't keep healthy boundaries or are you

Get to a place where your heart only zings for the kind of man who will cherish you.

aggressive and unable to respect the wants, needs and desires of others? Do you take everything too personally? Are you needy or overly independent? Are you feeding a hole in your soul with drugs, alcohol or too much shopping? Do you work to excess? Are your finances in shambles? Have you become a sloth?

Take some time to focus on yourself or at least be aware of your challenges. Relationships work much better when you own your junk. In other words, recognize when you're getting triggered by your significant other but understand that it's not really about them all the time.

I'll be the first to admit it; I have abandonment issues. There are times when I feel anxious and worried. My first instinct is to focus on my husband and what he's doing to create this feeling in me, and then I want him to fix it so I don't feel like that anymore. If I weren't self-aware I could start making unrealistic demands on him or react in anger at his perceived wrongs. But I know this about myself and he knows too. This awareness helps us maneuver through this issue in a more healthy way. He can take a few extra measures to help me feel secure but ultimately we both know it is my issue to deal with. I have to own my junk and be aware that sometimes triggering my issues is not really about him, or his job to fix. He can't make the feelings leave me. It's my job to work through them.

As I've said before, I've done it all wrong in the past myself. With Eric, though, I attracted a different kind of man. I was different. I am different. In the past I was fiercely independent. A level of independence is good, of course, but I took it to a whole new level. Abandonment issues make it more difficult to lean on others. I wanted to feel fully capable of taking care of myself and proved that that was so constantly. As you can probably imagine, that didn't really leave room for a *Real Man*.

I definitely put up with more than I should have for too long in many relationships from high school forward. My past experiences in various relationships include verbal abuse, control, forced physical intimacy, stalking, and even a few instances of being locked in places against my will. Now, I did not cause the behavior, I don't own that. But I was tolerating it by staying in relationships that featured these behaviors too long. And when you remain in a relationship with a man who is not good, you are not available for a *Real Man* who is.

The bad relationship experiences I endured left me with lower self-esteem. I needed to work my way back to feeling good about me. I also needed to overcome the fear that I'd end up in an unhealthy relationship again, to be able to trust myself to choose well and know that I'd take action if I needed to.

I also fell prey to the desire of hearing I was beautiful, looking for validation in a man's reaction to me. I needed to let go of control, be less independent and put God in control instead. I still worry some but not nearly as much. I don't have to be the planner, the visionary for decades of life. I can take it one step at a time, knowing God's got my back.

And I definitely found my way to a place where I *wanted* a man but didn't *need* a man.

I did not have God at the center of my relationships before. I did not realize he is a wonderful matchmaker. This relationship with God in the center is different, not without challenge of course, but better than anything I could have imagined.

So part of this process is about becoming aware of, and taking responsibility for, your own shortfalls, your own brokenness. As the saying goes, "own your junk." We all have it! If you need help with the process of recognizing, owning, and managing your own junk, stick with your CARE Group for encouragement, speak with a spiritual mentor, a coach, or seek assistance from a professional.

Life is a journey and where you are today is just a moment in time.

There are some basic strategies here that can help you to prepare for dating in the right frame of mind. Some involve simple changes that you can make immediately and practice. Others involve avoiding common trip ups I've experienced myself or have seen clients encounter. At the end of the chapter is a list of additional options that can help you work through deeper hurts.

The good news is that God has given us his precious promise to transform our hearts and make us new again. Life is a journey and where you are today is just a moment in time. Life does not need to stay the way it is and your past need not define you. If you are not happy begin the transformation now.

> *²⁶ I will give you a new heart and put a new spirit in you; I will remove from you your heart of stone and give you a heart of flesh. ²⁷ (Ezekiel 36:26-27)*

> *¹⁷ Therefore, if anyone is in Christ, the new creation has come. The old has gone, the new is here!* (2 Corinthians 5:17)

I encourage you to take note of what is wonderful about you. Are you solid in your self-esteem now or do you have some preparation to do? Refer to your Companion

Workbook to find additional questions and food for thought.

Single Mom Moment: Creatively Find Time for Dating

How will you create time and space for dating? The reality is, getting to know someone well will take some time. As a single parent you may have to be creative to carve out time for dating. The right man will find a way to have good conversation, spend time and share experiences with you.

I still remember the day Eric asked me what dating me would look like with kids in the picture. I had been asked the question by other men and gave that same response. "I'm not really sure. I don't have much free time, especially without my kids." To him I added that dating would probably involve time talking on the phone. Since he already knew my kids we could hang out with them together as well. We could have planned outings for when the kids are with their dad every other weekend. I don't really use babysitters often. I won't design a life that has me feeling like I'm missing out or pressured to spend less time with my boys. If

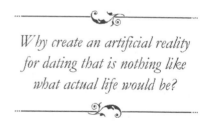

Why create an artificial reality for dating that is nothing like what actual life would be?

you want a life of spontaneity and frequent nights on the town I'm not the right fit. I really have very little wiggle room in my schedule. I said, "You will probably need to fold your life into ours to spend time with me."

Pretty romantic, huh? The thing is I had done the work. I knew what the reality was. And I knew to my core that I was fine with or without him. I wanted a man but I didn't need a man. I was already loved. The truth was that if he wanted to get to know me bad enough, wanted to pursue a relationship with me, wanted to see if there was potential, he would be creative and find a way, so he might as well see the real us. I say "us" because my boys and I were a package deal.

Why create an artificial reality for dating that is nothing like what actual life would be with us in a long-term relationship? A forever relationship with me needed to work for them too. And that meant a man who was willing to spend time to get to know them as well, a man willing to step into the role of stepfather with both feet, full force. I was not interested in halfhearted attempts at befriending my boys just to humor me. The right man would act out of a desire to know them, not only out of obligation.

And Eric figured out a way. We continued to do many activities with my boys, or we had long phone conversations after they were in bed. Sometimes he would come over to watch a movie with me. I still remember one particular night when he called and asked about a movie. I said, "My basement is flooding. I'm having to suck water with a shop vac about every 20 minutes and use the carpet cleaner to pull water out of the carpet." He immediately replied, "Would you mind pausing the movie in between? I can help you suck water. I'll bring another shop vac."

We found a creative, less than glamorous, way to bond over a shared experience that we still laugh about.

Again, I ask, why create an artificial reality to attract a man who may not be ready to sign on for what's true? By being authentic, I allowed this man to make an informed decision about what he was really in for, and I got to see the heart of a man pursuing me through the realities of a single mom life.

A first step in preparing is to know yourself and your circumstance. The second step is being confident enough in yourself to be real. Your situation is what it is. Land a man based on your reality not some drummed-up fantasy life that won't exist if you move forward.

Trust me, you want a man who is willing to dive in full force into your world. A man ready to partner with you on everything.

Forgive

Does forgiveness need to be a part of your preparation? Yes. Bitterness, anger, frustration, and hatred are all energy-sucking emotions and are often associated with how we feel about an ex or others who've hurt us in our lives.

An important part of my healing process was the intentional act of forgiveness. Forgiveness doesn't mean that what someone did is okay. It does mean letting go, ending the bitterness and reducing the anger.

As they say, holding resentment is like drinking poison and expecting the offender to become ill. It will continue to impact you and have an effect on your current and future relationships.

Forgiveness certainly didn't happen overnight! As a matter of fact, it didn't even enter my mind for a very long time. To be perfectly

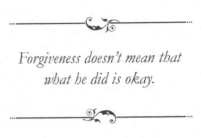

Forgiveness doesn't mean that what he did is okay.

honest, for the first few years after ending the relationship I delighted in the things that went awry in his life. I collected his struggles and failures like little affirmations and thought to myself, "Yep, I made the right choice."

I will never forget the day that I was receiving some healing prayer from the man I aptly refer to as "Gary Prayers". I was told, "you have to forgive." Ugggghhh!! A nice secondary effect of my continued anger towards him was that it had provided me a layer of protection for my heart. Stopping to think about him as a broken human being was too close to empathy. Empathy lives very close to love and I did not want to feel any feelings that even remotely resembled love for him. That chapter was closed and I needed to protect myself.

Truth was, I really didn't have anything to worry about there. I had successfully removed myself emotionally from him over the course of those years of healing, but I continued to find comfort in the idea of that extra layer.

The act of forgiveness was very difficult. I didn't want to let go of the practice of collecting his failures, which were also my affirmations. As is always the case, however, forgiveness turned out to be a gift to myself. It took a lot of energy to hold on to the negative stories. And empathy is okay. It has softened my heart. It has not led to the kind of love you feel for a partner, but to compassion.

Forgiving continues as a daily choice, with ongoing experiences to add to the challenge, but I am getting better.

The truth is, we are all broken.

So does part of your preparation need to include forgiveness as well? Maybe it's yourself you need to forgive. The same concepts apply. Whatever you did that led to the demise of that relationship, whatever choices you made that led down an unintended path, it was you in your brokenness leading the way. The questions you must ask are, what have you learned, what will you do differently going forward, and will you forgive? Are you ready to release your past?

The reality is, you can beat yourself up while you live the consequences of your actions or you can give yourself grace as you embrace your current circumstance. From a place of grace you have more energy to devote to creating a better life.

A focus on forgiveness releases you from bitterness, anger and frustration.

> 📖 *44 But I tell you, love your enemies and pray for those who persecute you. (Matthew 5:44)*

> 📖 *Hatred stirs up strife, but love covers all offenses. (Proverbs 10:12)*

> 📖 *Bear with each other and forgive whatever grievances you may have against one another. Forgive as the Lord forgave you" (Colossians 3:13)*

A related idea is that we can either ramp up the fight, or stand down and help the conflict quiet. Not from a place of fear. It can be a show of self-discipline, restraint and courage to remain calm against an aggression.

> 📖 *A soft answer turns away wrath, but a harsh word stirs up anger. (Proverbs 15:1)*

So how do you forgive? Here are some steps to follow. The steps are simple but the process can be very challenging.

Accept that it happened. After an event, and while we are very angry, we spend a lot of time thinking about all of the ways the situation could have been different. Why didn't he do that? This should have happened instead. If that was going to happen he should have done this. It takes a lot of mental energy to think of all of the alternative or preferred outcomes, the paths that could have been taken but weren't. These thoughts fuel more anger.

It is part of the grieving process, but at some point you have to embrace what happened. Those other things could have happened but they didn't. He could have made a different decision but he didn't. It is what it is. Considering the alternatives does you no good because you can't re-write history. Accept what is so. Avoid wasting energy on wishing it were different. Harness that energy and move forward from there.

1. **Hear the Other Side:** There are always two sides to a story and, at times, wildly different perspectives. It can be challenging, but if given the opportunity, truly listen. Try not to interrupt. Make an attempt to see

the situation from another point of view. You don't need to take on blame if they try to inaccurately reassign it, but do listen for nuggets of wisdom or a new perspective that makes sense. Sometimes hearing can increase understanding. Is there a way to find common ground or work through the challenge together? Can shifting your perspective heal the hurt a bit? Is there validity to any part of what they share?

2. **Be Appreciative.** Can you be thankful that you found out when you did? What did you learn? How will you do things differently in the future? Did you gain a new friend or strengthen a relationship? Does the action validate a decision you made in the past? In every circumstance is something positive and placing your focus there will help.

3. **See the Good**: Can you still see value in the person? Try to separate the good they bring from the bad thing they did. Weighing the pros and cons will also help you determine whether you'll leave them in your life or release them.

4. **Find Empathy**: Chances are high that the person who created the hurt is a hurt person. How does their brokenness negatively impact their life? Being empathetic doesn't excuse the bad behavior, but can provide a reason. Empathy can help you find a softer place to put this experience

5. **Express Your Feelings**: It can be difficult to share our hurts with the offender. If you are able and they are willing, it is a great exercise in healing. Do

consider how they might respond and set your expectations accordingly. If they have difficulty admitting fault don't set an expectation of hearing an "I'm sorry". You'll just feel disappointed. Instead create a goal of being heard. If you worry that they may be combative, have another person there as mediator or choose to write a letter instead. The act of writing your thoughts is helpful whether you ever send the letter to them or not.

6. **Give Yourself Grace**: Maybe someone cheated on you and you've been beating yourself up for trusting. The reality is that in relationships there are vulnerabilities. You have to let your guard down to let someone else in. He chose the behavior, not you. Maybe someone stole from you or took advantage of you. You might feel like you should have figured it out earlier, but at least you had the insight to figure it out when you did. So, you didn't realize as soon as you would have liked, you tolerated behavior longer than you should have, overlooked red flags that should have signaled the transgression. That doesn't make the infraction your fault.

7. When people harm you, take advantage of you, lie, cheat or steal, the bad choices are theirs to own. Beating yourself up about not anticipating the wrong does you no good. Part of forgiveness, whether you've played a part of not, will always include an element of forgiving yourself for any blame you assign yourself.

Getting over the hurt and moving on must include

placing blame where it belongs and giving yourself grace. Are there lessons to be learned for you? Probably. Take those with appreciation and let go of the rest.

8. **Design the Relationship Moving Forward**: Depending on the offense and circumstances, this person may or may not be out of your life. If you intend to maintain the relationship or must, get clear about any new parameters, rules or boundaries. Forgiveness does not require that you continue with status quo. Healthy boundaries keep us safe. Determine what you need in order to feel safe and whole in the relationship. It might mean the person is out of your life altogether or that you limit time with them. Maybe you'll ask for space for a period or avoid direct communication. Perhaps you need additional access to rebuild trust. You get to have a voice in the design of the relationship moving forward and should not feel guilt for any change you require.

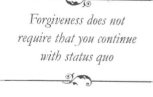

Forgiveness does not require that you continue with status quo

9. **Pray**: If it's not your thing that's totally fine. However, if you are a praying woman or want to give prayer a try, asking for God's help in this area is highly recommended. Pray that He will help you change your heart and see the situation through His eyes. Pray to have discernment and wisdom. Pray for His guidance through next steps. Pray to express sorrow to Him for your lack of forgiveness. Pray to

have your offender gain wisdom, insight and healing.

📖 [27] *"But to you who are listening I say: Love your enemies, do good to those who hate you,*[28] *bless those who curse you, pray for those who mistreat you. (Luke 6:27-28)*

Create a list of people you need to forgive. Use the steps outlined to begin the process. Share with your CARE Group. Pray for God's help if you are comfortable. God, I release it all to you.

Here is an example of what you might pray.

God, thank you for all you do for me. Please forgive me for my unforgiveness. Please help me to see this situation through your eyes. Please help to change my heart. Help me release the anger and hurt and to finally forgive.

Fracture Your Fears

A conversation shared with a single mom years ago illustrates well the fear that many women have about dating after they've hit a few snags or bumps in the road.

She approached me and asked, "Do you have a few minutes? I really need to talk!" "Of course," I responded. She frantically continued, "I don't' know what's happening to me. I'm having these feelings that I think I've not had before! I was on the Internet this morning looking up the warning signs of falling in love and I have a lot of them! I don't know what to do!"

I love it, "Warning signs." She was 100% serious and

completely unaware of what she was actually saying. It was her gut level, fear-based response, unfiltered.

As I've said before, few of us maneuver through dating without going through some kind of relationship trauma. And, dating with kids just ups the ante. Even if you've got the self-worth challenge figured out, the fear continues; "What if I mess up again?"

To this I answer, "And what if you do? Are you okay now? Will you be okay if . . . ?" To both the answer is, "yes." You may have some well-ingrained, valid fears around dating. Your healing process must include moving through them. I'll provide some simple strategies to work around such basic fears. If yours are more challenging I encourage you to find help for your healing.

- Ultimately, most dating fears center around these themes;

- What if it doesn't go well?

- What if he takes advantage of me?

- What if he rejects me?

- What if I'm not good enough?

If you can get to a place of trusting yourself most of these fears go away. Trust that if things don't go well you will be fine. Realize that if he does reject you, this does not decrease your value, and is a gift. All is well. If he does take advantage of you, that says much about him and little about you.

Fear can stop us dead in our tracks. And yet many of us share the same basic fears. The only difference, really, is our reaction to the fear. Some of us are stopped by fear, while others step around or bust through it. The more you let fear stop you, the smaller your life gets. Dating is an activity that can really ignite our insecurities. Here are some of the key shared fears:

Fear of Failure: Obviously, it is a lot more fun to succeed than to fail. But, if you are taking risks and putting yourself out there in dating, or in any other areas, you will probably have times when you don't quite hit the mark. If your fear of not meeting your expectations stops you from even going for it, your chances of finding your forever- someone go down exponentially!

Here's what I encourage you to do. Think differently about any dating experience that didn't end the way you would have liked. You don't *have* to title it a failure. Instead chalk it up to a learning experience, or be thankful that you figured it out, or for the discernment to know immediately that someone wasn't right. Thank God for keeping you safe from what might have led to great heartache or physical harm. Be grateful that you didn't waste more time than you needed to.

You have it in you to move past this one – go!

Fear of What Others Will Think: This one can be paralyzing in all aspects of life, especially dating. You don't want to meet him because, what if he doesn't like you? What if he doesn't find you that attractive?

The irony of this fear is that most people share this one. The man you are going to meet is likely experiencing the same fears. As you walk into the restaurant feeling self-conscious about what you look like to your date or what he is thinking about your clothes or your breath, all that he's probably thinking is – exactly the same thing!

So, instead of worrying about what he's thinking, how about focusing on what you think. Is he good enough for you? Is he attractive on both the inside and out?

And, if he does conclude that he's not going to continue dating you, this does NOT mean that you aren't good enough. It just means you weren't a fit for him. In the absence of facts to the contrary, you can decide that he obviously thought you were the most awesome person on the face of the earth but he was not worthy of your awesomeness! I mean, why do we always think "rejection" means something negative about ourselves?

I wish there were some magic dust that would make our fears go away. Unfortunately, the only way to overcome them is to bust through the very thing that stops you. Sometimes you can approach this breakthrough with small steps, other times you just have to hold your breath and go for it.

Years ago my oldest son, then 10 years old, was preparing for a show for our church. Part of the audition for the part was to climb a very tall ladder, which he did with ease. The cast and crew had been rehearsing for several weeks but didn't have the set built until days before. Though he had known all along that he'd be in a harness and climbing high above the stage, it wasn't until the set was built and in place that he realized just how high he would be, and reality set in quickly.

That night he lay in bed anxious. "Mom, I don't think I can do it! I'm too afraid."

I encouraged him by explaining he had two choices. You can decide the fear is too big, quit and move on, never knowing whether you could do it or not. Or you can bust through this fear and experience the exhilaration of achieving this goal despite it. You'll be safe. You'll be in a harness and they would not do anything that would risk harm to you.

The next day I let the director know and they got him up in that harness away from the set and just played a fun game of catch as he swung around high above the stage.

He began to have fun and started laughing. The fear he had created in his mind dissolved as he felt the security of the harness around him. He succeeded in busting through his fear and did great in the show. In that short time, he actually got so comfortable at the top of that set that looked like a giant haphazard stack of packages topped off with a tilted chair, that they had to remind him to *act* scared.

He felt so good about that achievement and can use it to this day as motivation to bust through new fears as they arise.

Similarly, your fears surrounding dating can either stop you in your tracks or provide the opportunity for breakthrough and a new found sense of achievement.

And, as with all challenges, feel free to pray for God's

guidance, security and courage. Turn all of your fears and worries to Him.

> 📖 *"I sought the LORD, and he heard me, and delivered me from all my fears". (Psalm 34:4)*

> 📖 *"Do not be anxious about anything, but in everything, by prayer and petition, with thanksgiving, present your requests to God. And the peace of God, which transcends all understanding, will guard your hearts and your minds in Christ Jesus." (Philippians 4:6-7)*

> 📖 *"Humble yourselves, therefore, under God's mighty hand, that he may lift you up in due time. Cast all your anxiety on him because he cares for you" (1 Peter 5:6-7)*

What fears stop you or slow the pace of your dating? Take small steps to bust your fears. Use your *Companion Workbook* to find more fear busting practice.

Examine Your Emotions

Emotions are good. They give us information. But they are different from fact. If your entire life is dictated by your emotions, you may be all

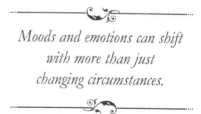

Moods and emotions can shift with more than just changing circumstances.

over the road. An emotional roller coaster is not amusing for you or those around you. Moods and emotions can shift with more than just changing circumstances. Sometimes we are just eating the wrong foods or lacking sleep, and without healthy boundaries in your relationships, your emotions can swing along with the people in your life.

Misaligned frustration taken out on a date mate can lead to unnecessary conflict that may require you to go into clean-up mode. And the emotion of anger can really wreak havoc. You probably already know this, but anger usually is not the real emotion. More often you are actually scared, sad, disappointed, or your ego might be bruised.

Anger can be a very toxic emotion. Too often we let it build up. One hundred tiny offenses left unaddressed to fester can create an atomic bomb-sized blow up. The spew will be aimed at the offending party, but can hit an unlucky uninvolved recipient. It could be the woman working the drive thru window.

Or, perhaps your habit is to react with huge anger for even the tiniest infraction. Small incidents made bigger can have you angry most of your day.

Are there times when you are reacting bigger than you need to?

Anger takes energy and is not fun to be around. The waitress forgot your drink. Is that really worth the incensed eye roll? Maybe you can give her grace and move on with your day.

I ask clients to consider emotions objectively. Never stuff them away, but don't treat them as fact. If your energy dips and you are having, "one of those days," know that it is your choice to keep it that way or not. Here's some food for thought:

- Is the focus of my feeling misdirected? Is there a reason beyond my current circumstance that generated this feeling? Have I been triggered by a past hurt, am I hungry or tired?

- Is there an alternative way to think about an incident? Maybe it's ironically funny rather than aggravating

- Is that small error worthy of your energy or can you let it go and move on? I always say, "Don't let anyone zap your joy!" Why let a small something put a damper on your day? You get to choose whether it does.

- Speak up when it's warranted. Don't let an accumulation of small things that could be handled one at a time build instead to create a volcano. How many great days are you losing as you collect those annoyances rather than address them?

- Create a rule. If I'm not willing to talk about it, then it must not be worthy of my energy to be mad. The Bible reveals a similar sentiment:

  📖 *A joyful heart is good medicine, but a crushed spirit dries up the bones. (Proverbs 17:22)*

  📖 *Whoever is slow to anger is better than the mighty, and he who rules his spirit than he who takes a city. (Proverbs 16:23)*

  📖 *But the fruit of the Spirit is love, joy, peace, patience, kindness, goodness, faithfulness, gentleness, self-control; against such things there is no law. (Galatians 5:22-23)*

Where are you letting emotions get the best of you? Do you have anger you need to release?

Grow Your Gratitude

In preparation for your dating life, it is also important to practice staying positive. It will keep your energy up and your motivation high.

Practicing the art of gratitude is not just about shifting focus away from what is hurtful, stressful or frustrating, or denying that those things exist. It is about purposefully placing an emphasis on things that are good.

If your initial thought is, "My life is filled with problems, what do I have to be grateful for?" I'm going to challenge you to dig deeper. In

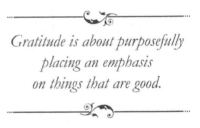

Gratitude is about purposefully placing an emphasis on things that are good.

every moment we have the opportunity to choose between a focus on what's going well or on things gone awry. Problems come at us and tend to command our attention. We must be more intentional in finding a focus on what is good.

We all take things for granted in our life and thus fail to feel grateful. If a doctor told you today that you would lose your sight within the next three months, how much would you appreciate your vision? What would you want to see often so the memory burned in your brain?

Do you think that perhaps the fact that you have vision today is something to be grateful for? I'll extend beyond the obvious to say that the items on the list of what you'd want to see and memorize are probably also things for which you could be grateful.

Consider starting a gratitude journal. Write in it first thing in the morning or at night before you go to bed. Or keep it in your purse or pocket to jot things in throughout the day. You will find your focus almost magically shifted, and it will become easier and easier to find positive things.

I have had times in my life when conditions were especially stressful. There were periods during my single mom journey when the weight of responsibility overtook me, or the stress of financial burdens created panic attacks at the grocery store. During these times I kept my gratitude journal right next to me all day, writing in it throughout the day or each time I thought of something else for which to be grateful. And it worked. Spending even a portion of a day doing that can shift your focus for a few weeks. For real, it is magical! Try it!

I also began having daily gratitude talks with my boys, as part of our bedtime routine. My boys would get pajamas on, brush their teeth and then climb into my big cozy bed. There we would take turns sharing what we were grateful for from the day. Sure, their lists usually included a game system or a toy but that's okay. Sometimes they'd throw an "I'm grateful for my mom" into the mix. We'd express gratitude for each other, our house, our pets, our car, family, friends, and food on the table. This fostered an appreciation for even the small things and events in life, so they would not be taken for granted.

I still remember the day my oldest, then no more than 8, told me that he wanted to write a book about gratitude talks. He wanted other kids to know about them and have gratitude talks with their moms because it would "help other kids going through a hard time to feel better."

When an eight year old feels inspired you know a simple exercise is powerful. So I encourage you to at least give it a try.

Still having trouble thinking of things? Here are some ideas:

- Beautiful day
- Rain to water the grass for free
- The transportation that got you to your destination
- Family
- Friends
- Eyes to see the sun.
- Your legs that carried you into the building
- Your co-workers
- The food you had for breakfast
- The trees and flowers
- The people who plow snow off the streets
- The teachers in your children's school
- The crossing guard who helps your child stay safe
- The roof over your head
- The bed you slept in last night
- Coffee
- Tea
- Your cell phone

- Internet access
- Your health
- Your kids
- Heat or air conditioning in your building

Gratitude is important in a long-term relationship too. It is easy to focus on flaws in our mates. Often what initially attracts you to someone can begin to grate on your nerves over time. Practicing a focus on gratitude in life will help you prepare for your forever-someone. You'll be purposeful about appreciating what's great about him.

> 📖 *"Be joyful always; pray continually; give thanks in all circumstances, for this is God's will for you in Christ Jesus."* *(First Thessalonians 5:16-18)*

Do you notice how joy is connected to giving thanks? That is how it works. Even in our most stressful moments there is an opportunity to shift focus towards something positive. We can always find something to be thankful for. And we can always thank God for His provision, His love, and His favor.

What are you grateful for? Make it a habit to practice gratitude every day.

Get a Grip in the Gap

Another potential for energy drain can happen when our expectations do not match our experiences. I call this "life in the gap" and it is where we spend most of our waking hours, whether we are aware or not. We travel through life creating expectations about everything and everyone around us. Our expectations are how we think things should be, how we assume they will be or how we want them to be. It can really be challenging in the dating world.

The problem is that our actual experiences rarely, if ever, match our expectations exactly, whether in dating or in life. Think about it. How often does anything turn out *exactly* as you thought it would? Sometimes the outcome is better, sometimes worse, and sometimes not better or worse, just different.

For example, you prepare for a vacation expecting to spend hours on the beach, only to experience terrible weather. Or, you start seeing a new man and feel the excitement of possibility only to find that he is commitment-phobic and spends most waking hours playing video games.

If we spend most of our life in the gap, much of our experience of life is determined by how we react there. The more we hold fast to our original expectations, the more opportunity we have for disappointment, frustration, resentment or outright anger which deplete our energy and make us less than wonderful to be around.

If, on the other hand, we can be a bit looser with our expectations, we are able to find more joy and fulfillment with the unexpected and may navigate through life mostly unaware that our expectations were unfulfilled.

To use a very simple and silly illustration I will talk about my hair. It is curly. If you know anything about curly hair, you know that it has a mind of its own. I really have little control over what it will look like each day. Regardless of what I am up to, how important the client, or the size of the audience I am addressing, my hair is going to do what my hair is going to do. If I held fast to a specific expectation of my hair looking a certain way for any given occasion I would spend most days very frustrated, upset or even embarrassed. Therefore, I must be flexible with my expectations of my hair each day, for my own sanity. The look of my hair is largely out of my control.

I told you it would be a silly example. Let's hit closer to home. I am sure you have been with boyfriends who do not meet your expectations. You feel like you have gone above and beyond for them and still they are not at all appreciative. They may have a sense of entitlement to your attentions, or maybe they experience no power in other aspects of their lives, so they assert some form of it with you whenever they can. Therefore, continuing to hold tight to an expectation that they will treat you differently is probably setting yourself up for disappointment.

To save your sanity and your energy, you must let go of such unrealistic expectations and recognize they are going to react how they are going to react regardless of what you think is appropriate. You can experience them as they are or you can feel frustration that they are not handling life as you believe they should, and, it is up to you whether they stay in your life.

In dating we can get tripped up in unrealistic expectations that add more challenge than necessary. Too many create the expectation that a man will be perfect and love will always be easy, then bristle at the first sign of struggle. Others view their man as a project and set about to "fix" him. The truth is we all have flaws and broken parts, so to expect anything different will land you in the gap. People will disappoint us. It's just the name of the game.

Fortunately, where people disappoint, God never does.

📖 *Whatever you do, work at it with all your heart, as working for the Lord, not for human masters,* [24] *since you know that you will receive an inheritance from the Lord as a reward. It is the Lord Christ you are serving.* [25] *Anyone who does wrong will be repaid for their wrongs, and there is no favoritism. (Colossians 3:23-25)*

Single Mom Moment: Realistic Expectations

Creating realistic expectations can be even more important as a single mom! Most single mothers are doing the work of two people so our expectations of ourselves and our lives must be aligned with this truth. If you began motherhood in a partnership you have to recalibrate. One of my many recalibrations centered on my pool. When I was a married mom of small children I stayed at home. I took great pride in our sparkly blue pool and had the time to tend to it. I vacuumed it often, checked the chemicals routinely.

Those first few summers as a single mom were rough in many ways. On top of it all, that previously perfect blue pool water was plagued by green algae. It seemed I couldn't get it right. It was usually swimmable, just not as pleasing to the eye.

Over time I got it under control. Not the pool -- that still isn't fully under control. What I did get under control, however, were my expectations about how that pool would look. The reality was that, given all the other things on my plate, I was not going to find the time to maintain it the way I'd like, at least not without sacrificing my sanity.

Similarly I found I needed some wiggle room with regard to prioritizing housework. Sure, I could set high expectations, but, that would only lead to frustration and disappointment. I chose instead to create expectations that were more aligned with my current circumstance, and to pick my battles more wisely. In doing this, I freed up more time for togetherness, good talks, and memory-making with my boys.

I still remember the time another single mom called with a late invite to watch a movie together. We chose my house, and as I hung up the phone I looked around. The main rooms were fine, but the laundry room and bedrooms were in disarray. I brushed it off and thought, we'll only be in the family room anyway. All is good.

To my horror she arrived and said, "I'd love a tour!" My mind quickly raced through the potential responses until I finally landed on, "Sure, let's go."

I believe I gave her a gift that day. You see, normally when we see others' homes, they are in visitor-ready mode. We then tend to compare our homes to that standard. She got to see the real us that day, and I'm quite certain she left feeling better about herself.

So, if you can't create realistic expectations for yourself, at least do it for your friends.

Watch Your Words

The way we process our life experiences and build relationships is through our use of language. The words we use provoke vision, emotion and sometimes even physical reaction, even if they are not spoken aloud, but just live within our thoughts. I recommend that you pay close attention to the language you are using with others, and in your own head and modify where necessary. This is an important concept for your entire life, but here we'll focus on of the language around dating. It will be important as you prepare.

Here's a quick illustration. I was speaking with a single woman who was describing a recent break-up. She lamented that all of her relationships result in her being abandoned.

Now, there are definitely relationship sagas that I would term as abandonment. I have my own share of abandonment issues, so I get it. However, the story she had just told, from an outsider's objective perspective, was actually one of triumph! She had been treated badly and broke off the relationship herself. From her account, it sounded to me like she had taken the appropriate action given the circumstance.

Yet, in her mind, this experience was being chalked up to another abandonment. Another relationship to add to the category of "I'm not good enough and people leave me."

I stopped her and said, "Is it possible for you to categorize this one differently?" I explained further: "As described by you, it sounds like you set some nice healthy boundaries for yourself, took charge and ended a relationship that was not good for you. That doesn't seem like abandonment to me."

She gasped and appeared shocked.

"How does it feel to look at it in that way instead?"

"Really good!" she exclaimed.

"And doesn't that feel more accurate?"

"Yes, it really does," she said with a growing smile. "Wow! I hadn't thought of it that way, but you're right!"

I watched as her whole demeanor changed. She had been in the habit of dubbing every failed relationship experience as "abandonment" and missed the opportunity to celebrate an instance where she was empowered and had done what was healthy to protect herself. It was a sign of her personal growth she hadn't even recognized because she was applying old words to new situations

Where else was she missing moments that could serve to bolster her energy and improve the image she kept of herself?

Our words are powerful. They create the framework for the experiences we have in our lives. Pay attention to the words you use and the stories you tell, even if just silently in your own head. You probably have some practiced, tried and true themes to the stories you tell. Are some of them no longer accurate?

What words do you say about yourself, whether inside your head or to others? Are they positive or cutting? It is not possible to turn off that little voice that speaks in our heads, sometimes too much. But we can change the context of those thoughts. So, perhaps the tape in your head constantly says you are stupid, ugly, ridiculous, unworthy, or fat. As you watch your words you can think within, "No, I don't accept that! I am beautiful, worthy and loved!" If it helps, surround yourself with visual reminders and encouraging words. Put positive words on your bathroom mirror or add a sticky note to your dash or laptop screen. Our lives can be filled with too many negative words so do what you can to surround yourself with better words from you.

Perhaps you are feeling like your options are limited right now. Whether it's a failed relationship, an unexpected expense, or feeling the drain of burnout that launched you to that place, you may have started to use phrases like "I have to," or "there is no alternative," or "you gotta do what you gotta do," which all leave you feeling powerless. Resignation sets in and locks you down, and you begin to feel like a victim to your circumstance.

The good news! I have a tried and true strategy that you can implement immediately, a simple shift that can change your perspective in a moment. It might seem silly but try it on for size. You'll be surprised at the dramatic difference it can make. Instead of, "I have to," adopt the phrase, "I choose!"

Powerfully proclaiming and owning the unhappy or less than ideal circumstance immediately empowers you. So, if you are hating your job right now and thinking, "I have no choice! I have to keep working here!" Change that phrase now and you'll find yourself in the middle of a reality check. The truth is, you actually do have choices. You don't "*have*" to keep working, or stay in that relationship, or stay in the living arrangement, or live in that city. You "choose" it.

You could make an immediate change. There might be some negative consequences to making the change, but you COULD just never show up to work again, you could move, you could leave that relationship.

The most obvious consequence of leaving your job, for example, is the lost income. It might be difficult to find another job while in transition, you might not be able to pay your mortgage or rent.

You could decide not to take that immediate action if your cost-benefit analysis has led you to conclude that it is better for you to stay right now. The reality is you are just CHOOSING not to make a change right now. There is a sense of freedom in that, isn't there?

Choosing isn't about giving full consideration to the alternatives. It's about realizing that the alternatives exist as an option and you *do* have choices, which helps you begin to use a different language to describe your current circumstance. Creating the alternative as a possibility can immediately generate a sense of freedom.

So proclaim it now! I Choose!

Living as a victim is not fun. Feeling empowered to choose your current circumstance allows you to stay, in a position of strength. It unleashes creative energy that you can then use to generate a plan of action to change the less-than-ideal situation.

I have shared this strategy with many clients who were on the verge of transition. Whether it was a change in job or relationship status, the simple shift in perspective helped them to choose the current situation, at least temporarily, and to move beyond the energy zapping feeling of being stuck.

Over and over I've been witness to the immediate change in attitude and the reignited energy that follows. From this empowered place they were able to table a swift, misdirected move while they contemplated objectively their next steps.

When you are communicating your dating goals or just thinking to yourself about your future, what words do you use? Do you say things like, "I will *probably* get married," or, "I *should* do that"? If you speak like this you might as well be saying, "I *won't* get that done."

And stay away from the phrase "I will try" altogether! There is no action in trying. Now, I do realize that I have asked you to "try it on for size" when considering a concept that is new to you and feels uncomfortable. This is exactly why the word "try" works there! It feels less threatening and doable to consider an alternative belief or action when we have not made any actual commitment to true change.

So, when you are actually ready to take action "try" is not your word. Using tentative language carries no power. No sense of certainty. You are letting yourself off too easily. Playing life to achieve requires persistent determination. The language you use needs to mirror this.

Instead, use words of action, certainty and ownership. Say, I *will* do that. And be specific. What will you do and by what time. "I procrastinated," rather

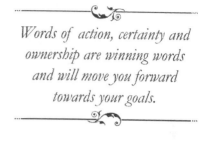

Words of action, certainty and ownership are winning words and will move you forward towards your goals.

than "procrastination happened." And, my personal favorite, "I commit to that," or "that is my commitment." We feel commitment in our bodies. So much more powerful than "I will try," yes?

Words of action, certainty and ownership are winning words and will move you forward towards your goals. They will transform your relationships.

> [29] *Do not let any unwholesome talk come out of your mouths, but only what is helpful for building others up according to their needs, that it may benefit those who listen. (Ephesians 4:29)*

> [8] *But now you must also rid yourselves of all such things as these: anger, rage, malice, slander, and filthy language from your lips. (Colossians 3:8)*

Spend time in your *Companion Workbook* to gain some additional self-awareness and key actions.

Build Healthy Boundaries

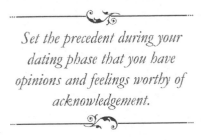

Set the precedent during your dating phase that you have opinions and feelings worthy of acknowledgement.

A healthy relationship with *Real Love* requires that both parties have a voice and a say in its destination. Healthy boundaries are the guidelines you should create together that will steer it successfully. Your dating life is setting the stage for your future. You want a man who will communicate his own healthy boundaries and who can respect your wishes and will focus on your desires. I am not recommending that you turn into a dictator or approach your relationships with a sense of entitlement. But do set the precedent during your dating phase that you have opinions and feelings worthy of acknowledgement. You also have legitimate needs, wants and desires.

You want to see how your date mate will react to your expectation of these things. Is he dismissive, a total pushover, or does he work with you to weigh each of your opinions to make a final decision?

If you have become the go-to gal who never says no, that is very convenient for the people in your life, but how is it working for you? Fix this one before you enter the dating scene. You need to have the skill of sharing your feelings. And, if others are designing your schedule with their requests you will not have time to date.

As I often say, you can generate more energy but you cannot make more time. So if you can't say no you will be overwhelmed. Moreover, if you are already overwhelmed, you are also carrying resentments towards many of the people in your life. You think they should know that you have too much going on. Well, they don't! Unless your life is filled with an unusual number of mind readers, they are not going to know unless you open your mouth and speak the words.

Saying "No" is an important skill that takes work for some. When you figure out why saying no is hard for you, you can begin that practice. Here are some of the key reasons many of my clients give for avoiding the word no. Do you see yourself in any of these descriptions?

- **Guilt:** You feel bad if you say no. People need your help. The truth is, maybe if you said no they would have some other resources to tap, or they'd figure out another way, or do it themselves. It might even provide them with a growth opportunity as they stretch themselves to achieve something without you.

- **You want people to like you:** You think doing things for others will require them to like you, and if you say no they will not. If this is you, it probably is true about your current friendships. You have probably become a magnet to people who base their relationships on what others can do for them. You don't want to attract this kind of man for your mate! The truth is that people who really care about you for you will like you regardless of what you *do* for them. Your relationships will become richer.

- **You need to feel useful:** If you are not doing for others, where is your value? This is a rough way to live. Your self-esteem and self-worth are based on others appreciating your selfless acts. Your entire focus is on finding people to assist. There is no room or time for focus on you or your own mission as you search for your next fix. And, at times, the people in your life are not appreciative of the work you've done. Or, the appreciation they share is never enough. You are disappointed and left wanting more. Then what?

- **You believe it is selfish to say no:** You believe that everyone else's needs are more important than your own and that self-sacrifice is virtuous. All of your time and energy is spent on others. You place no value on your own wants, needs or pursuits. This begs the question, "If you do not place any value on your needs and pursuits, then who will?"

- **God wants you to serve others:** Yes, God does want you to serve others with your gifts. His desire, however, is that we serve according to His plan. If you are filling your life by responding to the requests of everyone around you, where is there room for God to design your day? Often, people who respond from this belief are overwhelmed, resentful and burned out from their service. Nowhere in the Bible does it say that you are to serve out of obligation or to avoid feelings of guilt. He also does not call us to serve until we feel resentful or become nothing but a shell of our former selves.

Quite the contrary, serving God's way will leave you feeling rejuvenated, purposeful, joyful and fulfilled. The serving isn't always fully comfortable. You may be pushed out of your comfort zone, doubt your abilities or feel weary but not resentful or bitter.

Here is a passage from Exodus that describes a community coming together to build a tabernacle. It's a great story. Over and over it describes participants joining forces as they felt moved. So, yes, serve. But you are not required to respond to every request. Be thoughtful and prayerful and say no where appropriate without guilt.

> [21] *and everyone who was willing and whose heart moved them came and brought an offering to the Lord for the work on the tent of meeting, for all its service, and for the sacred garments.* [22] *All who were willing, men and women alike, came and brought gold jewelry of all kinds: brooches, earrings, rings and ornaments. They all presented their gold as a wave offering to the Lord. (Exodus 35:21-22)*

Some may find it difficult to state needs. Here are three necessary steps to building your healthy boundaries:

Create: Decide what you want from your relationships and life, and design rules or guiding principles that help you achieve your goals.

Communicate: If you don't let others know your boundaries, it is difficult for them to respect them. Chances are quite good that a date mate will not be a mind reader. Communicate your boundaries as you get to know one another or as issues arise. I created a rule for myself years ago that really helps me. I am not allowed to be upset if I haven't given someone the opportunity to make an informed choice aligned with my wishes. This motivates me to speak up. If I'm unwilling to exert the energy to share there's no need to exert the energy of anger. By sharing there is also room for negotiation where appropriate.

Keep: Keeping boundaries means providing gentle reminders or allowing for natural consequences. It doesn't mean keep at all costs. Remember, a healthy relationship requires mutual respect for each other's boundaries. That means not getting defensive or angry or taking it personally if someone sets a reasonable boundary that you feel infringes on your desires.

If you are new to setting boundaries, it can be difficult to keep them at first. Here are some quick strategies that you can implement immediately to help you keep your healthy boundaries.

- **Buy Yourself Time:** If someone makes a request that infringes on a boundary and you are apt to say yes immediately regardless, give yourself time to think before you respond. The key is to make sure that you actually follow through with an answer, though. Do not use the delay as an excuse to avoid answering altogether. That is passive behavior and you do not want that.

  - Let me check my calendar.

  - I'll get back to you in a couple of days.

  - Let me think about that.

  This extra time can also create the opportunity to reach out to a member of your CARE Group. Get their objective guidance and support for your answer.

- **Create Policy Statements:** Policy statements sound official, as though the decision is cast in stone and is completely out of your hands.

    - I have a policy to stay home on Sunday evenings.

    - I have committed to doing no more than five hours per month and I've hit my quota for the month.

    - I have already committed my budgeted dollars for the month.

- **Know Your Priorities:** Know your priorities ahead of time so that you can stick to them.

    - I'm sorry. I need to say no this time.

    - My number one focus is on (name the priority) right now. I can't this time.

- **Keep It Simple:** No long-winded explanation or excuses. This just makes you sound defensive. Practice stating your case and then stop. Continue to use good eye contact.

    - I'm sorry, I can't.

    - I won't be able to this time.

- **Tackle Easy Situations First:** Start by saying no to the paperboy or the phone solicitor first. Practice with members of your CARE Group. Build the muscle on the easy ones, then tackle your overbearing relative, then you are ready to apply the exercise to your significant romantic relationship.

Sometimes when we first begin to speak up we are fearful. That can make your voice shake. But, who cares? Speak up anyway. It gets easier and easier! You will be saying no with finesse before you know it.

One of my favorite quotes:

"Speak Your Mind, Even if Your Voice Shakes."
Maggie Kuhn, social activist, 1905-1995

I also encourage clients to treat boundary conversations as a request rather than an order. It's a softer way of asking for what you want and provides opportunity for some negotiation. That's what you want in a partnership with your forever-someone.

You can also use this communication formula;

When you_____
I feel_____
I know_____
Can you please_____?

So, you might say, "Joe, when you are late for our dates I feel frustrated and disrespected. I know it's probably not even about me and I shouldn't take it personally, but I do. Can you make an effort to be at least a few minutes early?"

In your mind you are thinking, "I am making a request." There is a distinction between a request and a demand. The demand can make your nonverbal communication very harsh and your result not as good. Thinking about it as a demand can cause you to avoid the conversation altogether because of worry over his response. If, instead, you opt for making a request, it will feel softer to him and more comfortable for you.

If you aren't dating anyone right now practice on some friends or members of your CARE Group.

📖 *³⁷ All you need to say is simply 'Yes' or 'No'; anything beyond this comes from the evil one. (Matthew 5:37)*

Where can you benefit from healthier boundaries? What skills must you build to create, communicate and keep them? Visit the Companion Workbook to find more to ponder on this topic.

Lick Your Loneliness

We are wired to live in community. Even as an introvert you want some kind of camaraderie, it's just more likely to be with one person at a time. So loneliness can ignite a yearning in us for connection. I have been there. I have already shared that as a single mom I was very lonely. It was a really challenging time. In talking with people, I find that many are feeling lonely.

Remember, you want to enter into the world of dating strong and confident, not needing anything. If you are in a season of loneliness I encourage you to make some healthy connections.

If you are like many people these days, Facebook or other forms of social media have replaced at least some of the in-person time you used to spend with friends. Those updates make us believe we're current on friends' lives and still connected, but it is at the expense of closer relationships. The loss of closer contact is an unfortunate outcome and can actually leave us feeling disconnected. I encourage you to reach out for real to those whom you are closest. Call or schedule a time to get together. Make it happen.

If you feel that your real, live connections are lacking, begin the work of creating new ones. What activities do you love? Find a group already participating and join in. Have you ever been on Meetup.com? You can find a meeting on just about any topic. Or, ask someone out to lunch at work. Talk to some of the moms during basketball practice. If you go to church, get involved or participate in a group there. Do you have a cause you'd like to support or a charity you feel strongly about? Devote some time to that. You may meet some great people with common interests.

And, of course, as I've suggested, take the steps in this book with the help of a CARE Group. If you don't know of one you can join, you can create your own. Doing this will establish new friendships and decrease your loneliness as you work to find your *True Love*.

The truth is that you are never fully alone because God is with you always. He is waiting patiently to be with you if you will open your heart and feel His love surround you.

📖 *So do not fear, for I am with you; do not be dismayed, for I am your God. I will strengthen you and help you; I will uphold you with my righteous right hand. (Isaiah 41:10)*

Do you have a strong community now or do you some work to do in this area? What actions will you pursue to reconnect or create new friendships?

Help for Healing

Healing is a process. I did not get to where I am by clicking my heels or snapping my fingers. In the process, I did find ways to experience joy, even in my down moments, even while I pursued healing with tenacity.

Diving into every possible aspect of healing you may need is beyond the scope of this book. You may need more individual support or professional help. Asking for help is not a sign of weakness. There is courage in accepting that you need help and power in the pursuit of healing.

Here is a list of some types of support you may want to try. I'm sure you can find resources in your area for many of these.

- Traditional Counseling or Therapy
- Theophostic Prayer
- Healing Prayer
- Life Coach
- EMDR
- Domestic Violence Counseling
- Alcoholics Anonymous
- Al-Anon

- Narcotics Anonymous
- Nar Anon
- Adult Children of Alcoholics
- Celebrate Recovery Program
- Grief Support Group
- Divorce Support Group

Principles of Dating Success

With your sights set firmly on determining whether a man is worthy of you, I'll remind you of the questions I asked you to pose about your date mate earlier. The ultimate goal is to feel good in the knowledge of who you are and standing on solid self-esteem *before* you pursue a relationship. Then shift your focus here:

Is *he* worthy?
Is *he* loveable?
Is *he* good enough?
Is *he* beautiful on the inside?
Is *he* okay?
Should *I* reject *him*?

Years ago I heard a story of the Eagle courting ritual. I am not sure where the line between fact and creative additions is drawn but it provides a wonderful illustration regardless. Eagles pair for life, similar to humans, so a female eagle takes great care in selecting her mate. She prepares herself before she begins and plans to spend time with many suitors before selecting her partner. Her expectation is set. She will not feel rejected if the first one, or two, or three do not work out. She plans to be patient. It is an important decision.

Many interested males will come to her. First, she will watch how each one flies. She will look for signs of strength and agility. If she likes one she sees, she will give him more time. Her next test is to see how he does fetching a stick from the air. She flies higher and higher, dropping the stick and observing his flight. Can he catch the stick? Is he swift and accurate with his flying? Does he demonstrate focus in flight?

If anything about him is not to her liking she abandons him and moves on to the next option. If he passes this test, however, she finds larger and larger sticks, increasing the challenge.

These tests are important. She knows that as her babies learn to fly they will fall from the nest. She will need him to swoop through the air to save them. She won't settle for just any male eagle. Her vision is set for her future. She knows what she needs in a mate. She seeks evidence that he will be a contributing member of her future family. His traits must be aligned with her vision.

Once she is convinced that he is worthy, then and only then will she commit to him for life and mate to create a family.

In sharp contrast, too many human females go through life begging, "Take my stick! Please take my stick!" For these, the only test is the man's acceptance of her and the results validate herself not her suitor. And too often the "mating" happens well before commitment. A woman will give away all of her power, minimizing her value. She says take my stick to prove that I have value, instead of saying fight for my stick to prove that you value me.

Remember the two women on the radio show fighting over the lying, cheating man with the sense of entitlement? The complete focus for each woman was on getting that man to take her stick. Neither took time to think about whether he was worthy.

I ask that you join the mission to shift this paradigm. Yes, you are in "competition" with women who are throwing their stick at men. But what are they really winning? Too many women do little to invigorate a man's desire to be excellent. While men are motivated by an ambition to attract women, too many women have made their prize too attainable, have set the bar way too low.

You are worthy of so much more! Make him work for it. Yes, you may lose a man to the women who are still

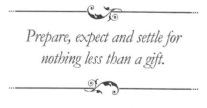

Prepare, expect and settle for nothing less than a gift.

giving it all up. But, again I ask, what are you really losing?

Take note of the female eagle and her process. You've made your list of criteria for a *Real Man*. You know his actions are more important than his words in determining whether he has the qualities you seek.

Don't compete for a booby prize! Prepare, expect and settle for nothing less than a gift. You are worthy of that. A bar set higher will elevate you above those looking only for a quick fix and will quickly weed out any man not interested in investing in a real relationship.

Single Mom Moment: Set the Bar High

Fatherhood is tough. Step parenting can be exponentially harder. There are almost always more complex circumstances surrounding. Be intentional about your choices and think about your children. Set the bar high for you and for your kids! Do not settle.

I've already shared how I was a different person as I started in my marriage with Eric. Now let me share how very different our dating relationship was, and why it was better than the way I'd dated in the past.

I believe that presence or absence of the 5 P's, the principles shared below, will give you clues to whether you are on the path to finding *True Love*. The 5 P's can help you initiate great conversations with your date mate, and help you to see the clues that he is authentically seeking to find his forever-someone too. I do believe that presence of these P's provides evidence of God's hand in the relationship and a man who is following God rather than just stating his commitment to Him.

Think of these 5 P's as the human version of "work for my stick."

Pursue

I believe that we are hard-wired with a desire to have a man pursue us. And men, the great hunters, are hard-wired to pursue. This does not mean women are weak. I have never been accused of that. But, even a strong woman wants strength beside her and will yearn to feel sought after.

I believe that God's design for dating is to put the desire in a man's heart for the woman he will love. Pursuit by a man proves interest and a

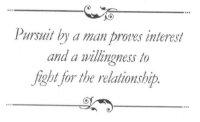

Pursuit by a man proves interest and a willingness to fight for the relationship.

willingness to fight for the relationship. If we pursue him we are just saying "take my stick" and won't know whether he's interested enough to work for our favor. Eric pursued me through our dating relationship. I want to share some specifics in case you have not experienced this kind of courting. I know that I had not. It required specific actions by him and I had to release control and just allow the relationship to unfold, a role that was definitely not the norm for this independent woman.

When my husband talks about the first time he laid eyes on me he shares that he felt a joyful presence around me. He didn't know anything about me, not even my name but had this urge to get to know me. I, on the other hand, was completely oblivious.

My oldest son, a 5th grader at the time, was in our Kensington Church Christmas service. It is always a very elaborate service, so this meant a big commitment of time for us, beginning at Thanksgiving. We lived a distance from the church so I would bring my younger son along as well and we would stay at the church during the entire rehearsal, a few hours several nights each week.

It was a very large crew and I was enjoying getting to know everyone. I had noticed Eric but didn't talk to him. Unbeknownst to me, he had noticed me and was trying to figure out who I was. He began checking around and learned that my other son was in the program. He began to work up the nerve to speak with me.

6 weeks of rehearsals and 12 services later we finally had our first conversation. It was Christmas Eve during the last service. We chatted briefly in the green room and learned that we had both attended the same University and had the same degree.

Eric loves to share that I then friended him on Facebook. To which I always quickly reply, "You and about 20 other people!" I had made a lot of new friends and did connect with many of them on Facebook.

Once connected, he checked out my profile and sent me a

message to ask about having lunch to talk business. We met up for our first actual conversation at an Olga's the first Sunday of the year.

That lunch turned into a slow, methodical pursuit that caught both of us off guard. We are not a likely couple. There is a 16 year age difference, though we didn't know that at first. I did know he was a lot younger and didn't hide the fact that I was older.

He started calling me periodically and asking me to meet for a lunch here and there. Sometimes our phone calls went well into the night as we chatted about everything and nothing. They were friendly chats. Nothing romantic.

He invited me to attend a small group presentation in his home for Financial Peace University. I told him it would be difficult to commit with my boys. He said they were welcome to come and hang out. Okay, great flexibility and accommodation. We would go.

He also started to invite all three of us to play games or to go kick a soccer ball around. I always happily viewed these as nothing more than play dates for my boys. I'd bring a book or laptop to occupy my time while I allowed Eric to bond with my kids. I saw him as a great role model and welcomed the time I got to relax and do my own thing while I watched them have fun. Finding time to sit and read a book was a rare occurrence. While he continued with persistence to invite me to join in, I, in complete oblivion, instead chose to relish in some me time.

Our phone calls were getting a bit more frequent and longer. We were just building a friendship and I was 100% letting him lead. Other than that initial Facebook friending he made 100% of the moves. I never once called him, texted or sent an email.

He periodically began inviting me to sit with him and his group of friends at church. One Sunday he saw me after service and said, "Oh! You were here! Why didn't you come sit with us?" I explained that if he invited me to sit with him I was happy to, but I was not going to assume it was an open invitation.

One Tuesday just before Valentine's Day we ended up at a gathering of Michigan State alumnae. We had a great time and spent most of the night talking about all kinds of things. He also invited me out for Valentine's Day. I, still oblivious said, "No, I'm just going to hang out with my boys."

On Valentine's Day he continued to pursue. It was my first clue that he was perhaps interested in more than just friendship. He called and said that he had a gift for me. He wanted to drop it off. He wouldn't stay, just "swing by." Since "swing by" meant a twenty minute drive each way, I kind of thought, "Hmmmm. Maybe he is interested." I was nervous. What was going on?

About an hour later my doorbell rang. I opened it to a card, flowers and a CD. No Eric. I peeked out the door and he was standing up against my garage door. He leaned forward and then ran up to the door. He said, "Don't worry. I'm not staying. I just wanted to bring you a little something and give you a hug. I didn't want you to be alone on

Valentine's Day." A quick hug, as promised, and he was gone.

During our next lunch he began asking what it would look like to date. He finally learned my age around this time. Despite the clues, he had assumed I was much younger. More food for thought and prayer for my young pursuer. There was no changing reality. Only time would tell.

I continued to let him pursue me. I still did not call or text. We had moved into the "talking" phase, as his generation referred to it. We weren't exclusive. We were still just getting to know one another and I left the pursuit of a relationship to him.

I believe that God designed dating this way. Our culture has created a dynamic where men have often become the hunted

While this may feed his ego it doesn't fuel his heart.

as women compete, push, shove and work for a man's attention. While this may feed his ego it doesn't fuel his heart. I don't think it's the way we are wired.

Let the man pursue you. Actions speak louder than words. Let his pursuit of you tell the level of his interest. If you jump in and begin competing for his time, are you just winning out of persistence or is he really interested? Are you morphing and changing and doing all that you can to drag him in like a fish on a hook or are you allowing him to feel an urge to find you?

If you are looking for your forever-someone don't you

want that someone to want you? Give them the opportunity to show you and work for you. Let them be the creative one that figures out what you love to do and finds a way to make it happen. And if it turns out that "he's just not that into you," that's okay. Let him go and move on. You are awesome and have so much to offer. Don't sell yourself short by working hard to earn the attention of someone who isn't pursuing you.

In this day and age it is so prevalent for a woman to pursue that a man may expect it and think you aren't interested in him if you don't. And some men are more shy and reserved and may need you to provide a bit of reassurance. If you are interested, let the man know that you won't contact him. It's okay to give a little encouragement but I recommend staying out of the relationship driver's seat. Avoid actions that push the relationship along or have you spending time together on your initiative.

It is a comforting feeling knowing that he is pursuing you. You don't have to question whether he's there out of obligation or because you pushed so hard. He's there because he chose to be. His pursuit gives a preview to the type of husband he would be. Is it done in a thoughtful and respectful way?

> 📖 *"Trust in the LORD with all your heart, and do not lean on your own understanding. In all your ways acknowledge him, and he will make straight your paths" (Proverbs 3:5-6).*

My sense is that women today are encouraged to be aggressive and competitive. Courting is seen as old fashioned and a woman who sits and waits on a man is considered too passive and controlled. I believe that if we take the time to listen to our hearts, we do want a man to pursue us. We want to feel wanted. We want him to work for us. We want it in our dating and will benefit from it in marriage.

The goal is not unbridled pursuit. A man should listen to you and respect your wishes and your boundaries. If you say you are not interested he should respect that and stop calling. If he isn't good at that, then lesson learned for you, celebrate the fact that you caught it early, and move on!

The beauty of letting him do the pursuing is that his efforts are communicating that he is interested enough to put energy into the relationship. And that's what you want; someone willing to work for you.

Protect

> 📖 *²³ Above all else, guard your heart, for everything you do flows from it. (Proverbs 4:23)*

Dating today often involves too many games. The intimacy dance, the truth trip-ups, the generate-the-jealousy game, the avoid availability act, the don't pick up, the wait to call, play the field. None of it is fun and seldom do these games lead to *True Love*.

Instead, find a man that will protect your heart. It is difficult to do. It takes honesty, will-power and a self-awareness. He must move the relationship with intention, communicating authentically along the way.

I can happily share that I got to experience this with Eric.

The entire time we dated, Eric sought to protect my heart. I always knew where I stood and what he was feeling about our relationship. He never left me guessing or wondering about anything. He did everything in his power to help me avoid that stress.

That's not to say that there weren't difficult conversations, uncomfortable topics or challenging circumstances. Protecting your heart isn't about shielding you from reality. It is doing everything in your power, as a man, to avoid making anything more difficult than it needs to be. It does mean having those tough conversations as soon as possible rather than letting anything linger unresolved.

As I've already shared, after we first met we spent several months just talking and spending time together. It was about a month and a half before he even brought up the subject of possibly dating. He was a man interested in moving towards marriage. In his mind he needed to see the potential for that before he moved forward with me. We didn't need to commit to marriage right then but it was important to feel that it was at least a possibility.

He knew that. He was up front about that. It wasn't some secret or hidden agenda. He was purposeful and self-aware. He was not going to waste my time or his if marriage was not a possibility. He wanted to be sure that the relationship was consistent with that path before he let my heart feel . . . anything.

He protected my heart.

So, we spent time as friends for about six weeks. Then we

started to discuss what dating might look like. We were each evaluating the situation. There was a wide age difference. I had two kids and an Ex. There was a lot to consider. We had tough but honest conversations before choosing to date. We were still not exclusive. We had just decided to spend more time with each other with the open knowledge that we were considering the possibility of taking our relationship to the next level. He did eventually kiss me and begin to hold my hand.

We spent time checking in with each other. How are you feeling about things? What are your concerns? What makes you happy? At one point he said he felt like we shouldn't kiss anymore. He didn't share specifically what was going on for him at the time and I still have never asked him. At this point it doesn't really matter. At the time, however, part of his analysis of the relationship had caused him to feel that kissing might be too much.

He protected my heart.

We spent time talking and getting to know one another for another three months before we decided to become exclusive. It was then that we also made our relationship public.

He still had never said the magical words, "I love you". He wouldn't even sign a card, "Love, Eric".

I waited and waited. I'm not going to lie, I was starting to feel frustrated. Really? You don't love me yet? Will you ever? But, I knew he was being very conscious of his actions. I appreciated that.

He protected my heart.

Finally, four or five months later, he felt sure and was ready to tell me, and my heart, that he loved me. He made it very special. He bought me flowers and recreated that first Valentine's Day hug. He shared not just that he loved me but also why. He said, "I didn't want to say it until I was sure."

He protected my heart.

With even the small things he never kept me guessing or waiting. I still remember our first Easter. It was prior to our commitment to be exclusive, so we weren't spending holidays together yet. I

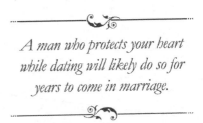

A man who protects your heart while dating will likely do so for years to come in marriage.

was with my kids and some friends, and he had gone to his parents. He realized that he left his phone at his parents' house and took extraordinary measures to make sure that I knew that he wouldn't be answering his phone for a few hours. He didn't want me guessing or wondering for even that short time about why he was unable to answer the phone if I called.

He protected my heart then, and he still does. I am cherished.

Dating life is your precursor to marriage. A man who protects your heart while dating will likely do so for years to come in marriage. A man who won't can be weeded out and released to claim a different prize.

Prayer

Whether you are a person who has never prayed before or someone who has made it a part of your daily routine I encourage you to make prayer a part of your dating life.

As Eric and I dated, we each prayed separately about what God's plan was for our relationship, and we prayed together for guidance and discernment. I remember the day that I got a very clear message. I believe it was from God. When I say message it wasn't an audible message but rather this knowing. It feels like a thought that pops out of nowhere. It can feel similar to a gut feeling but I find it's more centered.

I told Eric, "I still don't know what the long term plan is for our relationship but for right now I feel that we are supposed to be like this," and I clapped my hands together tightly and held them there. "We are to stay tight together and the current goal is to learn from one another."

On our wedding night after the ceremony and reception, the very first thing we did when we got to our room was drop to our knees to pray . . . together, as one.

We met in the church community, we stayed God-centered while dating, praying was meaningful to us, we prayed for each other and God gave us to each other, and so praying together on the most important night of our life's journey together was the most natural and beautiful thing to do.

I believe that God is a great matchmaker and has a wonderful plan for each of our lives. If we aren't connecting with Him we can't benefit from His wisdom and His vision. He loves us. He is not scary or interested in making us feel guilty. He just wants time with us. Wants the best for us. Is there waiting. So pray.

Pray for your date mate.
Pray about your date mate.
Pray to receive signs about God's plan for this date mate.
Pray with your date mate.
Pray to thank God
Pray for health
Pray for wisdom and discernment
Pray for God's plan for your life.
Pray. And then listen.

I still remember the call I got from a friend who was going through a non-dating related life challenge. She spent a lot of time in her car daily and shared, "I pray the entire time I'm driving! I pray and pray and ask and ask and pray some more but I'm not getting any answers." I laughed and said, "It sounds like you are doing a lot of talking! Have you taken any time to listen?" She started laughing immediately. "Oh, my gosh! I am talking non-stop and forgot about the hearing part."

That's the really cool thing about prayer. It establishes a relationship with a being who loves us unconditionally and wants nothing but the best for us. He just wants to hear from us and wants the chance to help us achieve His design for our life. A great strategy to help you tap into His vision is to pray and then listen.

If you are new to prayer, first, don't worry. God loves to

hear from you. There is no required formula for having a conversation with Him. However, if you do feel more comfortable with a set format here is a simple one to follow.

Praise God
Thank God
Ask God

You can also try a Listening Prayer. It means exactly what it sounds like. You pray and ask and then listen for God's response. In this busy world it is difficult to find quiet time, and often when we pray we do all of the talking and forget to listen.

To begin, you praise God and give him thanks and then ask your questions. I like to use a nice journal and two colored pens. I use green for my questions and purple for God's answer. I write the date and my question and then listen.

📖 *Therefore I tell you, whatever you ask in prayer, believe that you have received it, and it will be yours. (Mark 11.24)*

📖 *²⁶ In the same way, the Spirit helps us in our weakness. We do not know what we ought to pray for, but the Spirit himself intercedes for us through wordless groans. (Romans 8:26)*

📖 *Pray then like this: "Our Father in heaven, hallowed be your name. Your kingdom come, your will be done, on earth as it is in heaven. Give us this day our daily bread, and forgive us our debts, as we also have forgiven our debtors. And lead us not into temptation, but deliver us from evil. (Matthew 6:9-13)*

Purity

I know it feels oh-so old fashioned to have a discussion about "purity," because that used to be how I felt about it. I used to think "how silly!" I rationalized that purity rules were created in a time before there was good contraception, when families didn't want the burden of an unplanned child, and so they made up rules to lock down their daughters. I told myself, today there is contraception. Sex is fun. I won't have any emotional attachments or any hurts. My sexuality empowers me. As I've said before, I've done dating less than optimally over time, relying on beliefs that supported my actions. In hindsight, and compared to what I get to experience in my relationship now, I can tell you unequivocally, I now believe I was wrong!

Nowadays, sex sells everything, and we are expected to sell ourselves as women. There is pressure, even at a very young age, to bare a lot of skin, wear tight clothes and be highly proficient sexually, without intimacy. High schools and even middle schools are plagued with the fall-out of teens sharing naked pictures. For too many girls it's seen as a path to popularity and getting dates. Boys share the photos and disrespect the girls who feel compelled to send the provocative pictures.

You are so much more than your body! The full essence of you is in your heart, soul and mind.

Nothing is left to the imagination. And all of it erodes self-esteem. Boys get their physical fix. Girl gets the guy but what does she really win? They aren't learning to get to know one another. We are living in a culture where intimacy and connection are subordinate to physical exploitation.

You do not have to accept that for yourself. You are so much more than your body! The full essence of you is in your heart, soul and mind. If you capture someone solely with your looks and physicality, the relationship will likely be shallow and provide no strong foundation on which to build.

As He always does, God has created guidelines to protect us from ourselves. They don't take away our freedom, they give it to us. Too often our own fears and uncertainties confine and limit us.

> *[18] Flee from sexual immorality. All other sins a person commits are outside the body, but whoever sins sexually, sins against their own body. (1 Corinthians 6:18)*

Don't practice purity just because the Bible says so. Practice it for the reasons God placed the concept there.

There are some practical, non-biblical reasons for purity. Sleeping around increases the chance of contracting a sexually transmitted

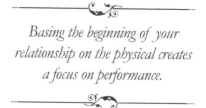

Basing the beginning of your relationship on the physical creates a focus on performance.

disease, which can range in severity from nuisance to life threatening. Even with perfect use of contraception, sex can still lead to an unwanted pregnancy.

But let's dig deeper for reasons that may speak more to

your heart.

Basing the beginning of your relationship on the physical creates a focus on performance. Your body, your techniques, your skill, the range of tactics you are willing and/or able to deploy, become the measure of your value in the relationship.

You are in the "what if he doesn't like me?" phase. You may feel compelled to do things you otherwise wouldn't. A man interested in only the physical isn't seeking to protect your heart, your esteem, or your body. And when your focus is on winning him with your physical performance maybe you aren't either. If you gave it all up the first time, what are you going to use as your encore? Perhaps you've been there with that morning-after feeling when you've done more than you normally would, or progressed more quickly than you would have liked. How does it feel? What questions are going through your head?

Was I good enough?
Is he using me?
Will he respect me or does he see me as a whore?
How will I keep his interest?
Will I even see him again?

Even if you feel like things went really well you wonder;

Will he still want to get to know me?
Will this relationship move beyond sex?
Is he sleeping with others?
How do I compare?
Will I even see him again?

I am continually shocked at the stories I hear on a morning radio show I listen to in the Detroit Metro area. They bring couples

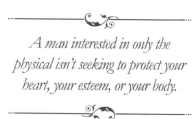

A man interested in only the physical isn't seeking to protect your heart, your esteem, or your body.

together who, for one reason or another, have not communicated since their first date and ask them, why not? I can't tell you the number of times I hear the guy speak badly of his date and some random flaws he found in her during their few brief hours. And, then, almost without fail, "oh, yeah, we slept together." I'm guessing this show is a fairly accurate representation of the sad state of dating life in general.

Maybe you give it up to him thinking it will make you special to him. In reality, though, his choice to sleep with you immediately says little, if anything, about how he really feels about you. Clearly the bar is not set that high for a man. You need to bring yours up a bit too.

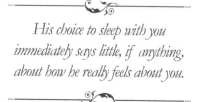

His choice to sleep with you immediately says little, if anything, about how he really feels about you.

If you are truly seeking to find that forever-someone, then sex alone is a shaky foundation to build on. It's a superficial transaction and not attached to our deeper relational abilities as humans. Even animals can enjoy a physical relationship easily. Humans have the capacity to connect on a much deeper level. In his book, *The Meaning of Marriage*, Tim Keller calls this deeper connection a "comprehensive attraction." It includes an appreciation for a person's "character, future, and mission in life." *(pg. 213)* The physical is so much more enjoyable, especially for a woman, when these other elements of the relationship are solid.

I can say from personal experience that dating with the physical relationship off the table as an option helped me to avoid worry. There was never any question that my boyfriend was there to get to know me. A guy can tell you anything he wants. He can easily tell you that he's looking for a relationship that leads to marriage. But, when you are engaged in a physical relationship with someone you are dating, you might be left wondering, "Is he here just for the sex? Is he having sex with others too?"

If, on the other hand, you follow up his, "I'm looking for a serious commitment" comment with, "That's great! So am I. I also plan to save sex for marriage." You will learn pretty quickly whether his actions match his words. If he was lying when he said he was looking for a serious relationship, he's outta there! What a gift! No wasted time waiting and wondering. Question answered and you can move on. And how much better does a break-up feel when you haven't already given him that part of you?

Without the pressure to be physical, you naturally have more time to focus on creating a solid foundation for the relationship. You aren't getting busy, you are getting to know one another. You are talking, sharing, creating memories together. You work on the emotional intimacy and friendship that will take you further than a physical relationship ever could. You are building the strong foundation that can weather the storm and stand the test of time.

Did you know that physical intimacy creates a chemical connection to another person? And, unfortunately for you, it creates a stronger connection for the woman. See, those feeling you feel after and the different response men sometimes have can be scientifically validated.

A prominent figure in neuropsychology, Dr. Daniel Amen, writes in his book, *Change Your Brain Change Your Life*:

> *"Whenever a person is sexually involved with another person, neurochemical changes occur in both their brains that encourage limbic, emotional bonding. Yet limbic bonding is the reason casual sex doesn't really work for most people on a whole mind and body level. Two people may decide to have sex 'just for the fun of it,' yet something is occurring on another level they might not have decided on at all: sex is enhancing an emotional bond between them whether they want it or not. One person, often the woman, is bound to form an attachment and will be hurt when a casual affair ends. One reason it is usually the woman who is hurt most is that the female limbic system is larger than the male's."*

The way chemicals are released in the brain during intercourse is very different in men and women, according to Washington Post reporter Laura Sessions Stepp, author of *Unhooked: How Young Women Pursue Sex, Delay Love and Lose at Both* (Riverhead Books, 2008). P. 129-130.

> *"While some young women can sleep with men and not become attached, many cannot. Scientists who study the endocrine system suggest one reason for that.*

When female mammals engage in intercourse, the hormone oxytocin is released in large amounts. Oxytocin, usually associated with the release of breast milk during childbirth, stimulates a caring instinct during or after intercourse, apparently more in women than men......Severing that bond can be difficult."

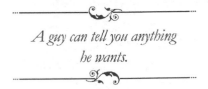

A guy can tell you anything he wants.

Casual sex is so common in our society today. It has diminished the meaning of sex in our minds, but our bodies and physical chemistry don't know the difference. So, you might tell yourself that it's all for fun with no expectation of commitment or even further contact. You may tell yourself you'll feel empowered, but the connection created by your body's chemistry, which is out of your control, can have you feeling otherwise. The chemical bond will lurk within your body regardless of what you have decided in your head. Meanwhile, for the man, with his more testosterone-induced response, it is more realistic to plan for a fun one-night stand without attachment.

That is why your brain says there is no attachment and yet you feel this pain deep down. You try to bury it. You might find yourself re-thinking the entire night, focusing on how it might have been different. You create this internal struggle as you fight to make the encounter playful while your body screams let's bond.

There is nothing chemically quick about a one-night stand. The interlude lingers.

You aren't going crazy; it's just your head fighting with the chemical induced connection in your heart. Well, technically, it's probably a connection in the limbic part of your brain. But, the specifics about that are beyond the scope of what I'll include here. Go check it out if you are interested in understanding more.

So, there is an emotional and natural attachment created between two people that is unavoidable and chemical based. It is in conflict with a culture of casual sex. There is nothing chemically quick about a one-night stand. The interlude lingers.

The Bible extoled this wisdom years before we could confirm it through science. We were warned to be careful about who we were intimate with because through the act we become one. The science of our chemical reaction validates this.

📖 *and the two will become one flesh.' So they are no longer two, but one flesh. (Mark 10:8)*

📖 *16 Do you not know that he who unites himself with a prostitute is one with her in body? For it is said, "The two will become one flesh." (1 Corinthians 6:16)*

If that person you have sex with is not available, emotionally or otherwise, or is not someone you would choose, you still may become chemically attached and go through a period of withdrawal. This can mean sadness, depression, decreased self-esteem. A yearning that cannot be fulfilled.

Don't you want to avoid that?

And the more accustomed you become to the thrill of the chemical response, the more challenging it becomes to put in the more rewarding but difficult work of building a truly intimate relationship.

Turning the physical act into a recreational activity goes against both our chemical makeup and God's intent.

God has created intercourse as a beautiful and physical expression of our emotional connection, a chance to be vulnerable and share this most intimate act. Our chemistry is perfectly designed to deepen and strengthen our bonds through this shared experience. Turning the physical act into a recreational activity goes against both our chemical makeup and God's intent.

You can also become hooked on the feeling of sexual release and feel less motivated to pursue a true connection. Or, your date mate may be in that place. The constant stimulation of new sexual partners and the visuals of pictures or porn may have stunted his ability to find interest in a more intimate relationship.

Dating with the physical relationship off the table leaves you open to focus on your real connection to a person.

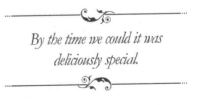

By the time we could it was deliciously special.

I can say from personal experience that it is wonderful to put the physical on hold until you lay that strong foundation. If you do, then the result is a deeper, more intimate connection, the completion of two lives coming together, a demonstration of love and a purposeful connection of two souls.

For us, waiting is also a challenging goal we created together and kept. A proud achievement. Disclaimer, I have never actually won an Olympic gold so don't know what that feels like, but in my mind, this feels like something close to that. Slight exaggeration, perhaps. But this was an achievement that, for us, was years in the making. We didn't meet, fall in love and say, "We're waiting until marriage, let's hurry up and get married." Our circumstance was a bit too complex for that. No, we dated for three years! It was challenging! We had to recommit often, pull back affection, sign contracts, and then create new ones to sign again. We deployed many strategies to achieve our goal. And we made it.

We both still celebrate the fact that we "can" be physical with each other now. We could have sooner, but we didn't. We waited. We said we "can't" for years. By the time we could it was deliciously special.

We continue to reap the rewards of that wait because, as we've found, if you wait you will continue to feel grateful for the fact that you can be physical for a long . . . long . . . long time! I highly recommend you wait for the extra satisfaction later.

Waiting also made the wedding and time leading up to our wedding night even more fun. We had an inside joke as we danced at our reception to a song by Pitbull ft. Neyo, Nayer & Afrojack that encourages giving it all up. Of course, we were ascribing a completely different meaning, the opposite, in fact, to the actual intent of the song, which encourages only a one-night stand, not a lifetime commitment.

What are your thoughts after reading this chapter? There are some key topics you may want to discuss with your CARE Group. And dive into your *Companion Workbook* as well.

Single Mom Moment: Role Model Dating

On top of what I've outlined in this chapter you have the added responsibility of being a role model to your children. As a single mom your dating life is on display for your kids. Do they see everything? Of course not. But, children always pick up on more than we realize. If you have a difficult time making good choices for yourself think about your kids and the kind of choices you would like them to make when they start dating. What do you hope will seem "normal" to them at that time? They are watching.

Partnership

The final important P Principle for dating is partnership. In a nutshell this means get real, own your own stuff, have great integrity, cover the tough topics don't avoid them, don't sugar coat them. Respect one another and work together toward common goals.

As you grow to know one another you share and design your relationship together. There are no dictators. If your date mate is not able to partner with you during this phase, chances are he's not a good bet for a future.

I will, once again, use some examples from our dating life to illustrate what partnership can look like as a relationship blossoms.

As I've said before, I definitely have abandonment issues. Too many people who were supposed to have loved me instead let me down. My heart has been broken and it leaves me on guard. But, I know this about myself. I know when I'm being triggered. I shared this with Eric when we were dating, not so he could fix it for me but so that he could keep it in mind, understand, give me grace, remind me gently that the feelings I was having might not really be aligned with whatever was happening at the moment. For my part, I work to avoid reacting when I'm triggered. He doesn't enable me but does consider how his actions may impact me because of this brokenness.

Partnership

I still remember the first time he gave me the gentle reminder. He was in Florida and had been calling and texting me throughout the trip. A single friend arrived to visit him and all communication stopped. Not for days, just for a few hours. It was a new pattern. Our relationship was new. I started feeling uneasy. Then the anxiety kicked in and I decided all kinds of things about what he must be doing.

When we finally spoke late that night I was agitated and

accusatory. "Why would you call me multiple times a day each day and then suddenly stop when your single, playboy friend arrives? I know what he's like. What have you been up to?" He responded calmly, "It feels like this reaction isn't really about me." He wasn't frustrated. Instead he gave me grace.

Partnership

As a single mom there are lots of ways to evaluate for partnership rather quickly!

I remember the first time Eric called to ask if I'd like to watch a movie with him. He'd bring it over once my kids were in bed. It was very early in our getting to know one another phase. He understood the fact that I couldn't leave my house at a moment's notice. Spending time with me meant coming to me, and he was interested enough to figure out a way to make it happen.

Partnership

As I've already shared, there was also the time he called with an invitation to watch a movie and I couldn't sit through it uninterrupted because my basement was flooding. Currently. And Still.

This was my life. Might as well lob it out there. No pressure - he was in no way obligated to help me in this situation. But he did. He said, "how about if I bring a movie AND a shop vac? Two's gotta be better than one. We'll just pause the movie every 20 minutes."

Partnership

The first time he came to my house for dinner was a last minute event. I had made spaghetti, which he was excited about, but my kitchen wasn't exactly suitor-ready. And my kids would be eating with us so it certainly wouldn't resemble anything like a date.

He still wanted to come. He didn't seem to notice the dirty dishes in the sink. This was my life. There was always something left undone!

My 5th grader stood up from the table and said, "Excuse me." Then walked around the corner to fart loudly. "Thanks for excusing yourself, Bud!"

Eric laughed and seemed to enjoy all of it.

Partnership

His mom was sick with cancer when we met. She was doing okay initially but her health began to decline. We spent time with her as she moved to a hospital bed in the first floor office of her home. When the terrible moment came when she lost her battle, we were both there. I was his strength as he grieved.

Her wish was to have an informal visitation right in her home after she passed away. I helped the hospice nurse clean up the space, added a beautiful comforter to the bed, brushed her hair, put a bit of makeup on her face and lipstick on her lips. She looked peaceful when her closest friends arrived.

Partnership

Partnership. It's each of you being there for the other. Each showing strength and jumping in. When one is always a mess and the other is always filling in the gaps, that is not a partnership. Partnership is a graceful give and take that exists when you are there for each other. A dance you do

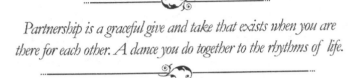

Partnership is a graceful give and take that exists when you are there for each other. A dance you do together to the rhythms of life.

together to the rhythms of life.

Is your date mate truly willing to meet you where you are? Will he dive into your life or does he require a lot of change? Are you walking together through life to celebrate the successes and work through the challenges? If so, your dating experience should begin to feel like a partnership. Find some additional thoughts to ponder in your *Companion Workbook*.

Progressing

There are definable stages in dating. In the beginning you are learning the basics about each other. It's the time for butterflies, anticipation and diving into the unknown. When you hit that first date you have no idea whether you'll even make it through one dinner with the man.

Generally, after that first date you know whether there is physical chemistry and whether you were able to carry on a conversation about the basic stuff of life. If you make it past that first hurdle you move to learning more about each other. Do you have some shared interests? Is he geographically desirable? Is he taking some initiative to plan dates and pursue? Do you enjoy your time together? What kind of relationship is he interested in having?

You each evaluate the relationship to determine whether it is worth the additional investment of time. Will you keep spending time together? Will the relationship become exclusive?

The next phase may bring the wonderful glow of infatuation. Excitement builds and you begin to dig a little deeper, learning more details about a potential partner. You are still putting your best foot forward and so is he. There is generally no conflict and topics of conversation are still mostly lighthearted. If there are any little red flags they are easily overlooked as you enjoy the giddiness of possibility.

As the relationship progresses beyond infatuation and things get a little more real, you start to delve into more meaningful topics, and to let your guard down. We'll call it simply the post-infatuation phase.

In the book "The Meaning of Marriage," at page 214, author Tim Keller recommends asking these questions to determine whether you have moved on from the infatuation stage of dating:

- Have you been through and resolved a few sharp conflicts?

- Have you been through a cycle of repenting and forgiving?

- Have each of you shown that you can make changes out of love for the other?

He believes that there are two kinds of couples that will answer no. Either they are a couple who has not experienced conflict and remain in the infatuation stage, where all is rosy, or they are a couple who keep fighting the same fight, over and over without resolution.

I'll add a third possibility: One or both partners is engaging in some serious people pleasing behavior and has failed to voice contrary opinions or desires. The other partner is running the show.

Flaws and quirkiness are apparent and can still be cute, but annoying in this phase. You might begin to share tasks such as meal preparation or picking up dry cleaning, and the general logistics of life. At this point Saturday night dates are probably assumed. You begin to feel an emotional attachment. The fear that investment won't realize a return begins to set in, while at the same time you are tantalized by a vision of a future that includes him. You begin to ask, either to yourself or to him, "where is this going?" The sense of urgency to know where things are going is generally greater in women, which is why I just say, "at this point have patience."

Patience

Maybe you are one of those people who flip directly to the end of a novel to see how it all turns out. From there you determine whether it's worth the investment of time to read and enjoy the pages leading up to the end. In essence, that's what many women are trying to do with dating. Is the ending of this story good enough for me to invest more time?

The point in a relationship when women begin to ask this varies, and the words each uses may differ, but ultimately what every woman wants to

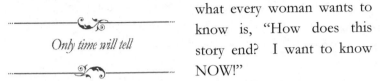

Only time will tell

know is, "How does this story end? I want to know NOW!"

Somewhere between these progressing relationship phases is where many of the singles I've mentored start asking the questions either directly to their date mate or just to friends;

Where is this going?
Is he being truthful?
Is he really this nice?
What are his faults?
Does he really like me?
Will he hurt me?
Is he the one?

To all of these I answer, "Only time will tell".

You just can't know it all in a minute. You have to let the story unfold before you can determine where it is going.

The pressure or desire to know the outcome is based in fear. If this isn't going anywhere:

- I don't want to be hurt.
- I don't want to let my guard down.
- I don't want to waste my time.
- I want to know if he'll cheat.
- I need to know that he's sincere.
- I want proof that he has integrity.

If your desire to learn the end of the story becomes too great you might begin to apply pressure to your date mate. You want evidence that the story will end well and seek confirmation and push for promises too soon.

Stop!

Only time will tell.

You can't start pushing for a relationship label only two dates into it.

You can't start giving ultimatums after 6 weeks to quell your anxiety.

Only time will tell.

And pushing reverses the pursuit, turning you into the pursuer.

Be patient. Only time will tell.

Practicing the art of patience is difficult in an instant gratification world! We want what we want and we want it now. Gone are the days of quilting circles where the satisfaction of a finished product was months away.

In today's world our expectations of time are calibrated by fast food restaurants, high speed Internet and 24/7 news brought to us real-time via television or social media. Our attention spans seem to shorten by the month.

Brian Regan, a great comedian, jokes about the two sets of instructions on a Pop Tart box. If you can't squeeze in the 3 minutes it takes to toast the pastry you can opt for the time-saving 3 second microwave option. As he puts it, "If you have to zap-fry your Pop Tart you need to loosen up your schedule!"

How often is our worry, frustration or disappointment the result of unrealistic expectations around time? "What's taking him so long?" "Why hasn't he decided yet?" "I need to know now!"

This kind of pressure and impatience does not add value to a relationship.

Instead of applying pressure to get to the end of the story quicker, focus on answering your own questions. Is this relationship right for me? What do I want?

And focus on the fact that you will be okay whenever or however it ends. The extra stress occurs from attaching the outcome of the relationship to your feelings of self-worth.

Remember, you don't have to do that to yourself. His actions say something about him, not about you. If he ends up cheating and you didn't anticipate it, that doesn't mean you're stupid. If he lies and you catch it, that doesn't mean you're gullible.

If the relationship doesn't become the fairytale that you'd like, you'll still be okay. You'll chalk this one up to a lesson learned, and move on a step closer to finding the right one.

Sit back and watch to see if his actions match his words, and enjoy the journey because you are on one, and only time will tell.

Paired Values

You have your list of core values. Once coupled, you are working through life together. Even under the best of circumstances, having much in common with your mate, there are still going to be areas where you must compromise and negotiate. This is where paired values are important.

Once again the Bible gives a great example that illustrates the importance of paired values.

> 📖 *Do not plow with an ox and a donkey yoked together. (Deuteronomy 22:10)*

When decisions are made there's the work of executing them, in harmony. It is very difficult to live life together while you are each pulling in different directions. That's why the yoke is the perfect illustration. You are tied together. You share the fruit and the consequences of your decisions together.

Go over your list of core values with your date mate. Are his well aligned with yours? If so, they can be a source of connection. If not, they can be a source of disharmony.

Here are some hot topics you should discuss with your potential partner as your relationship progresses. The goal is to find synergy and paired values.

Core Values: You should already have these outlined. Ask your date mate to go through the same exercise with the same list to see whether your core values are well aligned. You certainly don't need to have the same values, but complementary values would be good.

World View: A world view supplies a comprehensive into what a person considers real, true, rational, good, valuable and beautiful. How do you each see the world? What is your perspective on the universe, the cosmos, humanity, history? What do you find stunningly beautiful? Where, for example, do you prioritize health of the earth and financial prosperity?

Life's Purpose: I often share that many people do the lazy river way of living life. They just bump along letting life's circumstances or the opinions of others define the course of their lives. Others choose to be introspective, pray, analyze why they exist and what mission they should be on. As you explore this topic with your date mate you will want to take note first about whether either of you has a sense of purpose. Are both of you just bumping along? That might be okay if you each feel satisfied. If one or the other of you has started to feel a deeper need for an objective or goal, that sense that there must be more to life, can you get on the same page about exploring or setting about to fulfill life's purpose? It can become a challenge if only one person has a passion for allowing purpose to drive life's decisions. If both of you are driven by your passion for purpose are your visions aligned, or will they possibly have you moving in wildly different directions through life?

Moral Code: How are definitions of right and wrong created? How strictly do you adhere to a moral code? What do you consider to be a big moral offense? What is a smaller indiscretion that can or should be overlooked?

Religion: During discussions on this topic cover more than just your religious beliefs. My husband and I mentored a couple interested in a marital path who were well aligned in their religious views, but each was very attached to and involved in their own church. The churches were very different. Neither was anxious to make a change, but this was a major element of their lives requiring negotiation in order for the relationship to move forward. Do you plan to practice your faith? What religion? Would you like to go to church regularly? Do you have a church you prefer? Do you like a big church or small church? Would you like to participate in any group activities? Will you attend only or are you interested in being involved? Do you want to raise your children in a religious home? What kind of religious teaching would you like your children to have?

Planning a Future

Some of these are not the sexiest of topics to discuss when you are carried along by romantic love, but sharing your expectations for the logistics of life with a potential partner is another important step in creating a solid future together. It is often these seemingly minor issues that can become the greatest challenges in a marriage. It's the stuff of daily life that can cause recurring conflict. Take time to talk through these questions. Document answers and concerns.

Extended Family: How do you define extended family? How deep does it go? I have some friends who define close family as all of the aunts, uncles and

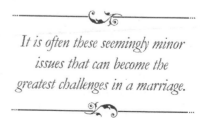

It is often these seemingly minor issues that can become the greatest challenges in a marriage.

cousins for several generations and also the extended relatives of in-laws. Even a birthday party for a two year old becomes an elaborate event. There is also constant pressure to participate in milestone celebrations for the entire clan. It makes for a very busy life. How often will you get together with family? Will you include them in birthday celebrations and Sunday dinners, or will you only see them for weddings and funerals? Which family will take precedent in the event of scheduling such occasions?

Holidays: Related to the previous item, how will you coordinate family get-togethers and share time? Will holidays be limited to your immediate family? Will you travel for them? Do you like to host holiday gatherings? Which ones? What is your favorite holiday? Do you like to decorate and purchase elaborate gifts, or do you prefer keep it simple for such occasions? How big are birthdays for the adults in your family?

Careers: Will you each have careers and if so, will one or both be time demanding? Will one or both of you work from home? Is moving for a career or job opportunity in the realm of possibility? What will the other partner do if a move is required? Will one of you forego a career to stay home with the children, or to care for an ailing parent, or to manage your home life, or retire early? Who will be the main breadwinner? Is income the main drive for career decisions or can passion for the work be emphasized?

Location: Where do you want to live when married? Do you prefer the country or the city? Will careers influence your locale, or will family and friends drive those decisions? Do you want to move often or set down deep roots?

Dream Home: What is your dream home like? Is it large or small? Traditional or contemporary? Is it a house or an apartment? Where is it located? Do you want land? Water or mountains? City or country? Seclusion or close neighbors? Is it important for certain amenities to be easily accessible?

Finances: Will you do a monthly budget? Are you a spender or a saver? Do you prefer purchasing with cash or credit? Will you have joint or separate bank accounts? Who would pay the bills? How will you pay for household expenses? Do you plan to save for retirement or education for your children? Do you buy or lease vehicles? How much outstanding debt do you have? How did you accrue any debt you have? What is the likely division of labor to be for managing the daily finances or the long-term investments?

I encourage you to find a Financial Peace University (FPU) study or something similar and participate together. In FPU Dave Ramsey provides a great foundation to help you create a solid financial plan and future. According to him, most couples are comprised of two types of money personalities; the Nerd and the Free Spirit. His strategies help you to respect and appreciate your differences while still working collaboratively to make money decisions. Learning before you start combining finances is a great way to go! Check with local churches. Many have small groups or offer classes. If his program isn't to your liking find something similar that will get you working through financial discussions armed with strategies and a solid plan.

Giving: Are you interested in giving time or money? Will you tithe? What causes do you care about? Would you like to travel to serve with your time? Are there any specific places you'd like to go?

Children: My husband and I actually had to work through this one and was another one of the "get real" conversations we had very early on, before we even decided to commit to a dating relationship.

Eric shared with me early on that he'd love to have 2 or 3 children of his own. I kind of tucked it back in my mind. At this point we were just spending time as friends and hadn't even discussed the possibility of dating. I would have been jumping the gun to bring up my reproductive status at this point.

Then, when we started to talk about what it would look like for us to date, I did bring it up. "If we are really going to explore the possibility of dating there is something you need to know. You mentioned one time in passing that you would like to have children of your own. Before considering whether you want to pursue a relationship with me you need to know that it may not be physically possible for me to have another child. It's not 100% out of the question but highly unlikely."

This was an important conversation to have that would color our entire future together. Again, I couldn't change reality, so why hide it. If I was going to engage in a relationship with someone I hoped to one day love, I did not want the foundation based on deceit or concealment of reality. Might as well lay my cards on the table right away so that he could make an informed decision.

How many children would you like? How long would you like to wait after marriage to start trying? How far apart will you have them? Do either of you have any known or potential reproductive challenges? If you are unable to conceive naturally what/if any options would you want to try? Is adoption or fostering a possibility? Would you like to pursue fostering or adoption regardless?

Parenting: So, there's the conversation about how many kids you'd like and then there's the one about how you'd like to parent them.

If he already has kids, that serves as a great window view on a potential future with him as a dad. I don't know who first said it, but you often hear in the world of recruiting, and from Dr. Phil, that "the best predictor of future behavior is past behavior." What role does he play with his kids now? Is he working hard to avoid child support, does he do only what's minimally required or is he actively involved in creating a good life for his children? Does he spend time with them, keep his commitments, and act as a good role model? Is he making great memories for his kids, or does he see them as an obligation or burden?

Many couples skip talking about how they plan to raise children, what kind of discipline they will use. Finding out too late that you have different ideas about what's best can create conflict over the course of years. If you both have children, the conflict will happen quickly. You can't run a happy home with separate rules for each family of kids, especially if both sets will be spending the majority of time with you. The blended family has additional complexity so it's best to have a plan ahead of time.

Will you want to nurse or bottle feed? Will you let the baby cry it out or hold them? How much structure would you like for your children? Will rules be flexible or strictly enforced? Will you have your kids learn age-appropriate chores? How involved do you want to be with their activities? Will either of you want to coach? Will you want to play chauffer? Do you want to volunteer at school or participate in field trips? Will you do only family vacations, adult vacations, or some of both? Once you are parents, how often will make time for date nights? If either of you already has kids, where will they live? How do you feel about allowances? Will they have to be earned, and how much is appropriate? How do you feel about discipline? What kind of discipline do you plan to use? How do you feel about spanking? Are children to be "seen and not heard," will they run the house, or be allowed space somewhere in between?

Single Mom Moment: Parenting as an Already Parent

It is important for every couple considering marriage to talk about children and parenting. With a single mom the stakes are already high. You already have set ways of parenting, and he may have different ideas about them. Does he even want kids? Because you have them, so you'd better be on the same wavelength about that reality. If you move towards marriage, he will be stepping into a ready-made family with set rules and a set way of living, he will be expected to love and parent children that are not his biological offspring.

Having this tough conversation may be difficult but it's

paramount. Your kids aren't going away. It's stark reality. You must get on the same page about how you will parent these kids together, or you will have a constant uphill battle.

You, like other couples, must also cover the topic of whether to add to the existing brood. What are your plans and what is possible? You know what goes along with pregnancy and taking care of a newborn. Are you up for the challenge again? Are you physically able to have more kids?

Friend time: How often do you each plan to spend with friends individually? How often would you like to spend time with other couples?

Entertaining: How much entertaining would you like to do? What kinds of entertaining do you envision?

Nights Out: What activities would you like to do together during a night out on the town?

Nights In: How do you envision spending your evenings in?

Physical Intimacy: How often? What activities are a possibility? What would you want to avoid?

Family meal times: How many nights a week would you like to eat at home as a family? Who will cook? What kinds of meals do you like?

Travel: How often? Will you take vacations together, or separately, or a mix? What about business travel? Will you fly, drive or do day trips and stay-cations?

Drinking: How often, how much?

Hobbies: What will you do together and what will you do apart?

Chores: Who do you anticipate will be responsible for what tasks?

Laundry and Ironing

Grocery Shopping

Meal Planning and Cooking

Car Maintenance

Home Repairs

Yard Work

General Household Cleaning

Heavier Cleaning and Organizing

Changing Sheets and Making Beds

Washing Windows

Partnership Pitfalls

No relationship is perfect, so remember that isn't the goal you are working towards. But once again, having awareness and working to improve is key to creating relationship success. In my years of mentoring and helping clients through relationship struggles I have identified some pitfalls that plague many relationships. If you determine that either you or your date mate are engaging in tactics that lead to such pitfalls, it doesn't have to be a deal breaker. It does mean you have some things to talk about and work through. If you're with the right person he'll be interested in improving and won't mind you calling him out, lovingly. The hope is that he'd be interested in improving and would welcome you as his accountability partner in making the change.

Similarly, if you identify your own behavior in these examples, then you have the opportunity to gain self-awareness, own up and grow, and to see if your date mate is willing to help you.

Conversations around these topics provide the opportunity to create a deeper bond if handled with compassion. If, however, either of you responds with anger or defensiveness, that is a red flag you must consider.

Hooping

Way worse than a pop quiz, hooping is a test you give your significant other without their knowledge. You use the results to gather information about your relationship. I call it hooping because that's the visual I get. You're holding the hoop and he doesn't even know he's supposed to jump. You are "hooping" him.

I see this often in the relationships of singles I mentor, so let me illustrate. You say, "I'm really tired tonight. I need a relaxing night at home."

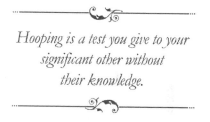

Hooping is a test you give to your significant other without their knowledge.

This is great if you are just conveying a feeling or opinion. It becomes a hoop if you are looking for a reaction from your significant other and then assigning your own meaning to his response.

In this particular hoop scenario, let's say the "correct" or desired answer is, "Would you like me to grab some carryout and come over? We can watch Netflix."

You don't *say* that you want that, however, because in your mind, he should just *KNOW*. If he doesn't give the "correct" response, you will make an assumption about what his response really means.

Assumptions are dangerous and generally not fact-based. For instance, if he says, "Okay. I'll just see you tomorrow then," you might decide that this means he's excited you didn't want to go out because he wants a night out without you. As a matter of fact, you may go on to assume, he's been hoping for an opportunity like this for a while. He'll probably cheat. Before you know it, you've doomed the whole relationship in your imagination.

Perhaps his actual thought was, "Wow, she's had a really busy week. I want to let her get her rest. I really miss her but I don't want to be pushy. She'll get some great rest tonight and I'll see her tomorrow."

Absent the hooping, you would probably just ask him if he'd like to come over for Netflix, or maybe ask a clarifying question to find the facts around why he quickly agreed to not go out that night.

Key characteristics to help you identify when a scenario is, in fact, a hooping:

- Failing to share information about what you really want.

- Pre-planning how you will feel based on potential responses.

- Assigning an assumed meaning or intent to the other's response, otherwise known as jumping to conclusions and treating them as fact.

I had a client whose husband held many hoops, all of which, if failed, meant she didn't respect him. Wow, was he an unhappy camper most of the time! He wanted to feel respected, yet he aligned almost every move she made to mean disrespect. Meanwhile, most of what she was doing had nothing to do with him at all. If she was delayed returning from grocery shopping, or went to a friend's house without realizing he'd hoped they'd spend a night alone together, he defined it to mean she didn't respect him.

Any strategy that lands you in the world of assumption is going to create challenges in a relationship. Hooping can be dangerous. You can be way off course with your assumptions. These assumptions will cause you to react and your reaction can shift the direction of the relationship, transforming an otherwise good relationship into a shaky one. And, for some reason, the assumptions are rarely positive, rarely lead to the idea that, "Oh, he must love me so much." No, hooping tends to take you to the dark place and feed your main fears; he doesn't care about me, he's going to cheat on me, he's trying to avoid me, he's going to break up with me. And on and on and on.

I had a short-lived jittery time in my relationship with Eric. He started doing his own laundry. The meaning I assigned to this was that he was trying to live more like a roommate than a spouse. My assumption about why he started doing his own laundry made me feel nervous. Was this the beginning of the demise of our relationship? Thankfully, I only allowed myself to feel like that for a very short time before I just asked, "Why are you doing your own laundry now?" The answer made a lot of sense. His clothes were getting mixed up with my boys' clothes and it was difficult to find them. He preferred to just do his own laundry.

Well, win – win!!

Had I continued to assume without asking, I would have continued to stress over nothing. My false perception could have altered the way I was interacting with him. Luckily we talked about it, causing that stress to disappear.

If you want a specific response or action ask for it. Don't use a secret test that only you know the "correct" answers to -- it will get you into trouble!

It is possible that, unbeknownst to you, your boyfriend could be holding hoops for you, so that you are a victim of false assumptions. Does your date mate assign inaccurate intentions to your actions or words and then react accordingly? Have you been failing some hoop tests? It's a good thing to identify and discuss. Whether you're the hoop holder or the hoop jumper you want them gone. They are not conducive to a healthy partnership.

Swooping

Swooping is a term I coined a few years ago while working with clients, to name a phenomenon I see often. It is the act of "swooping" in to fix, save, smooth over, or come to the rescue of another person. Done periodically, it can be an act of love or necessity, but living your life this way is enabling. If you or your partner needs constant saving there is probably some opportunity for personal growth.

Here's the problem: We know that suffering the natural consequences of one's behavior is a motivator for changing it. It's a basic parenting principle that applies to other relationships too. But if someone is constantly swooping to the rescue, so that consequences are avoided, then the behavior and its resulting problems or issues, are never addressed or changed, and the motivation to do so is lowered by the expectation of rescue.

In working with swooping clients over the years, I've found that often they swoop without even being asked. That means they are on constant alert, and shifting responsibility for another's success on a whim.

Constant swooping can also signal control issues. You want things a certain way. You'll jump in to make it happen.

A swooper's intentions may be good, but the positive affect is probably short lived. They are fixing what's wrong for the moment without addressing the underlying cause of the problem.

Let me give you some examples that range from the simple swoop to the heroic save:

- He shops too much and needs a few extra dollars to cover living expenses. Every month.

- He forgets his phone a few times a week, and you swoop on over to pick it up and deliver it to him.

- He drinks to excess and is too hung over to get up, so you clean up, hide the truth, and call his workplace with a creative excuse. Again.

A relationship with a swooper is under constant pressure, because it allows unhealthy behavior to continue. And the swooper risks sliding into a parent role to their partner as they fix, save and control. There is nothing sexy about that. Avoiding this one is important.

Stringing

Another common relationship pitfall is attaching strings to actions, promises or words. Stringing is a form of manipulation. I will do something for you but I expect a specific action from you in return. Which really means, of course, that I'm not doing it for you, but rather, in exchange for something I want from you. For instance, if I go to church with you, I expect you to get a babysitter and go out with me afterwards. Or, if I stop drinking, you need to move in with me.

Stringing is problematic on a couple of different levels. First, it can lead to a lot of score keeping. It's a lot to keep track of when every action requires a reaction of equal or more value. Eventually either or both of you will often feel slighted or hurt.

Second, stringing leads to actions or words that are not done for the right reasons, but simply to obtain a reward. Over time you've set up a couple's currency system. In a strings-attached relationship there is no selflessness. Every request fulfilled is actually done with the thought of "what can I get out of this?" That is not a *True Love* relationship; it's a constant trade-off.

How does this play out in a dating-for-keeps scenario? This way: If going to church together is really important to you,

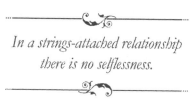

In a strings-attached relationship there is no selflessness.

but not to him, chances are he will not continue to go to church with you once he has you for keeps. He is doing it to achieve an end goal. It is not a part of who he really is. He can't sustain the "favor" over a lifetime. And you will one day fall short in compensating him.

Worse, stringing can become a form of manipulation or punishment. I won't do this for you because you failed to do this for me in the past.

Now, there are times when we can negotiate as a couple in a healthy way. That is different from strings. There is give and take where both end up with the benefit of the bargain -- a win-win that is enjoyed by both. A favor or act of service given out of love is done without strings. The difference lies largely in intent and whether there is an ongoing score card or couples currency attached.

Remodel Motivations

If this pitfall exists in your relationship it may find you falling for the man you wish you had rather than who he really is. Remodel motivations help you assume you can change a partner and has you minimizing the red flags you see.

Too often the end result is a woman falling in love with

the *idea* of the man. She sees him for his remodeling potential, whether he shares that vision or not. Maybe this is where that term rose colored glasses originated. You skim over both minor and glaring faults to see the "if only" version of him, and wow, is he wonderful:

- If only he had a better job.
- If only he lost some weight.
- If only he drank less.
- If only he wasn't so angry.
- If only he went to church.
- If only he played fewer video games.
- If only he appreciated me more.
- If only he was less into hunting.
- If only he was a better communicator.
- If only he dressed better.
- If only he spent less time with his friends.
- If only he was interested in marriage.
- If only he wanted kids.
- If only he wanted to spend time with my kids.
- If only he'd overcome that addiction.

And you think to yourself, "Someday he will." The problem is, you can't base your future on a plan to fix or transform someone. In the dating world there are no fixer uppers. A man is not a piece of real estate. You don't look at him and say, "Well, he's got good bones. Just needs a little updating and a facelift." He's not an inanimate object just waiting for your remodeling touch.

During your dating life a man will likely be on his best behavior, meaning that's probably the best you can expect. Rarely is it the start of an uphill climb to improvement. If

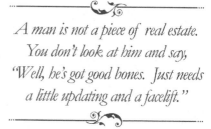

A man is not a piece of real estate. You don't look at him and say, "Well, he's got good bones. Just needs a little updating and a facelift."

you consider moving forward in the relationship with thoughts of, "Well, once we're married, I'll be able to change that," you are setting yourself up for frustration and possible failure. Instead, remove the rose-colored glasses and base your decisions on what already *is* versus what *might be*.

Consider your "if only" list again. Change the beginning of each sentence to "he won't" and then see how you feel. This might be your reality. How important are those changes? Do any of them become deal breakers when you look at them like this?

- He won't have a better job.
- He won't lose some weight.
- He won't drink less.
- He won't be less angry.
- He won't go to church.
- He won't play fewer video games.
- He won't appreciate you more.
- He won't be less into hunting.
- He won't be a better communicator.
- He won't dress better.
- He won't spend less time with his friends.
- He won't be interested in marriage.

- He won't want kids.
- He won't want to spend time with your kids.
- He won't overcome that addiction.

Now, is change ever possible? Of course! His priorities may change with time; he might have an epiphany, find new interests, mature. But he might not. Some of what you define as "faults" may just be who he is, how he was wonderfully made. For instance, maybe he doesn't like crowds and prefers quiet nights at home. He could be an introvert who will never joyfully accompany you to that big party.

For true change to occur, he must want it for himself and have the personal motivation and ability to make it happen. Otherwise, even if he says he'll change, he might just be saying it, or temporarily changing, to make you happy. He might not be as interested in making you happy once he's won you. As wonderful as you are, you may not be enough motivation to sustain the metamorphosis for a lifetime.

If your plan is to somehow bring about the changes from the driver's seat of his life I'm asking that you reconsider. He won't want you there and you'll start to feel like a mom to him. Over time he'll build resentment and you'll have the frustration of trying to control what you can't. It's a huge responsibility to try to steer someone else's life, and is almost always bound to result in disappointment.

The unfortunate truth about change is that it is hard. Sometimes even simple adjustments are not swift. Even with good intentions, you don't always do what you know you should. Think about your own life. What have you been unwilling or unable to correct? Almost everyone has at least a few. You intended to get in shape and work out routinely, but haven't or couldn't stick to the diet your Doctor recommended. You meant to finish that certification, but time got away from you. You made a commitment to quit smoking but still have a few cigarettes a day.

Chances are you have not been a perfect steward of your own life, so why would you want the added burden of being responsible for someone else's? Sometimes it's easier to focus on the faults of others than to face any disappointment in yourself.

Another trip-up potential in the remodel motivations pitfall is to focus on *why* he's making what you consider to be bad choices. You may spend time determining the root cause so you can define his fix.

The problem is that focusing on why keeps you from seeing him clearly as is and may result in your lingering in a relationship that you don't really accept. You spend time figuring out why the behavior exists rather than how you feel about the fact that the behavior is there.

Furthermore, sometimes when you think you've nailed down the why you can begin to recognize it as an excuse for the behavior and tolerate it longer. It's

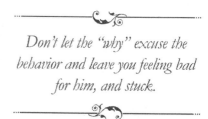

Don't let the "why" excuse the behavior and leave you feeling bad for him, and stuck.

important to see the why as a reason not an excuse. This is an important distinction. Don't let the "why" excuse the behavior and leave you feeling bad for him, and stuck.

Here's a hypothetical illustration of what I mean. He is unwilling to make a commitment to you. You are sad because you really love him. You know he'd miss you a lot if you moved on and feel that his losing you would be one of the biggest mistakes of his life. You stay in the relationships and get sidetracked into finding reasons why. You rationalize:

- He doesn't have a good relationship with his mom.

- His first girlfriend cheated on him.

- It's his age.

- His angry outer self protects his highly sensitive inside. He's so afraid of being hurt.

Even if you've nailed the why it shouldn't excuse the behavior or mean that you must tolerate it. His reasons may be sound and you may feel bad for him. That doesn't require you to stay in the relationship. If all of your assumptions are true he still has the option to overcome his past adversity and commit. But, in this hypothetical situation, he's choosing not to commit. If this is the case it ultimately doesn't matter that you have figured out why. It doesn't matter that *you* feel losing you would be the biggest mistake of his life. If he's not worried about it you shouldn't be either.

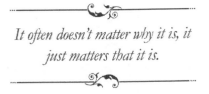

It often doesn't matter why it is, it just matters that it is.

It often doesn't matter *why* it is, it just matters *that* it is. That's where you need to be, especially in the early stages of the relationship. If you have little invested you have little to lose.

Ask yourself instead, "How do I feel dating someone who is unwilling to commit?"

You could be applying this pattern to anything from your "if only" list. He gets to choose who he is and you get to do the same. If each of you is happy with the other, as is, you should move forward. If not, move on.

If he does decide to change it can't be just for the sake of keeping you or making you happy, because then, in his mind, you become responsible for whatever struggles he encounters in relation to it. If you hear, "I'll do this if you stay," this is a string, his motivation is you, and that won't end well

I've seen women leave a relationship and then get sucked back in as he begins to take the right steps. Almost without fail, the man reverts back to his old ways. He got the prize. No more work necessary. Humans don't tend to exert more energy than necessary to get what they want.

At some point you might not be a big enough reward to motivate or maintain the change. If it's still all about you, he'll revert back. By that point you will have invested more time in a relationship that is probably doomed.

True, sustainable change happens when there is personal motivation for a better life, and a plan to make it happen. To determine 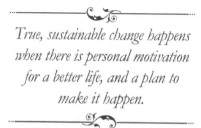 whether the motivation is solid, look for concrete actions aligned with fulfilling the plan rather than just accepting the possibly well-intended promises of change.

In dating, most often your best bet is to assume that what you see is what you get. So, get real about what you can live with and make your decisions from there. Avoid those remodel motivations and the love for an "if only" man.

Removing your remodel motivations to accept someone as is becomes a gift you give to them and yourself. You release them from your feelings of frustration and disappointment and you enjoy a renewed focus on designing the relationship based on what is rather than how you wish it were. Do you need to set some better boundaries, spend less time together or cut ties altogether? An accurate vision will help you make decisions more aligned with reality.

Is there someone you can accept as is now? How could or should the relationship be transformed? You'll find some additional thoughts to ponder in the *Companion Workbook*.

Relentless Mistrust

Relentless mistrust, also known as jealousy or the green-eyed monster, signals trouble in any relationship. Years ago I was dating a man I didn't trust. I found myself testing and checking. I wanted to trust. I needed to trust. It was uncomfortable feeling so uncertain all the time. I kept thinking that at some point I would either have enough proof to trust him, or I would catch him at something and know for sure I shouldn't. There was cause for concern and I was caught in limbo land.

A friend then gave me this wise advice. "It doesn't matter

whether he's actually trustworthy or not. If you can't trust him you shouldn't be in a relationship with him." She was so right!

Either I wasn't ready at that point and had some work to do on myself, or my gut was giving me a warning I should heed.

Sometimes mistrust is warranted. Throughout this book I've emphasized the need to see that words and actions match. Integrity is key to a lasting

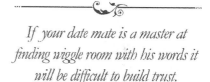

If your date mate is a master at finding wiggle room with his words it will be difficult to build trust.

relationship. If your date mate is a master at finding wiggle room with his words it will be difficult to build trust. Can you be certain that you are catching 100% of his lies? Doubtful. How many more are you missing? Even if you only catch him in little "white lies" those can be a slippery slope to bigger untruths. Where does he draw the line?

Are you sneaking to check his cell phone daily? Worrying about what he's up to when he's at work? Do you require him to prove he's trustworthy on a daily basis? Has it become a never ending test?

I certainly don't recommend trusting a date mate 100% without some passage of time and some evidence that he is a good risk. "Only time will tell." If they build a good track record, however, at some point, you have to decide that they are worthy of your trust, let your guard down and become vulnerable.

If you can't do that, maybe you need to own that the mistrust is your issue to fix, not his. Maybe he can never be available enough, transparent enough, or trustworthy enough to quiet your fears because it is your fears that overshadow everything, not his failures.

Then you need to turn the mirror towards you, because this is really about lacking trust in yourself.

- Trust that you will be okay if he does let you down.

- Trust that you will take the required action if he doesn't have good integrity.

- Trust that you will have the wisdom and discernment to figure it out.

- Trust that you make good choices.

- Trust that you are worthy of great love.

- Trust in your instincts that you've given it the time required to believe in him.

- Trust that if he is deceitful it is not your failure.

- Trust that you will be okay regardless, that you are strong enough to endure.

- Trust that God's got you and loves you no matter what.

Remember, his bad behavior is not a reflection on you. His ability to get away with it for a time does not mean you are gullible or dumb.

Over time, your lack of trust and constant accusations can lead to a self-fulfilling prophecy. At some point he might say, "Well, she thinks I'm doing it anyway." Or, "I can't keep putting effort into proving myself." Even a good man can tolerate only so much.

Maybe you are the one on the receiving end of relentless mistrust. You can be extra transparent to some extent to alleviate his fears, but if he truly has issues it won't be possible to do enough to quell his fears. If you stay in such a relationship, you risk subjecting yourself to constant scrutiny and control. Be aware and be ready to apply the brakes and shift the ownership of the problem back to where it belongs. And then add this to your list of items to assess as you decide whether you'll move forward in the relationship.

Centered on Self

As I've stated before, I believe that little toddler screaming, "Mine!" still lives within us as adults. And in today's world that voice seems to have gained momentum. "What's in it for me?" is the common cry.

Our world seems fueled by desire for money and material acquisition over everything else. Morals and personal values are not often what garners praise. These are symptoms of a morphing societal norm that is validating that toddler within.

In a *True Love* relationship you want to feel served, cared for, loved and cherished. But for this to happen, both partners in a relationship need to have an outward focus, a desire to serve, negotiate and make sacrifices for the relationship. There must be an ebb and flow to the give and take between partners. Where both individuals can't win, the relationship must.

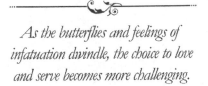

As the butterflies and feelings of infatuation dwindle, the choice to love and serve becomes more challenging.

The outward focus may not be how we are wired, but each partner must commit to it. It isn't enough for a flash of inspiration to hit. No, the motivation to serve must come from your desire to put your mate first. Your dating life is giving you information about, and setting precedent for, this aspect of a potential married life too.

You might not always feel like making him dinner or asking how you can help. And as the butterflies and feelings of infatuation dwindle, the choice to love and serve becomes more challenging. Love isn't just a feeling, as they always say. Love is choice in action. It's a choice you make to honor each other, a gift you each give to serve.

Being selfless in love does not mean becoming a doormat or hiding your own wants. It is about considering the other person and finding ways to serve them, not out of obligation, with strings attached, or in a way that builds resentments, but from a place of service in love. An act of service coming from a place of love feels very different than a strings-attached gift that will have you creating a couple's currency.

I highly recommend the books of Willard F. Harley, Jr. In this subject of service in love and others, he provides a wealth of information to help you sustain a wonderful union. In one of his books, "His Needs Her Needs: Building an Affair Proof Marriage," he outlines a great formula. I'll provide only a very quick synopsis here.

Over the course of years counseling thousands of couples through their marriage challenges, Mr. Harley was able to identify 10 basic categories of need that, ideally, are met within the marriage. Meeting a need or sharing a positive experience makes a love deposit in one's love bank account.

According to his findings, individuals who are unable to get basic needs met in the marriage may innocently seek fulfillment of those needs outside the marriage. Needs provided

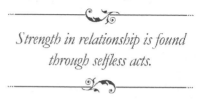

Strength in relationship is found through selfless acts.

by someone other than a spouse lead to love bank deposits, which, whether planned or not, can lead to feeling attached or to an affair.

As he queried couples, he also learned that women and men tended to prioritize the list of needs in the opposite direction. So, in general, what is high on the list for a man is low on the list for women.

What does this mean? This means that in order to continue to make love bank deposits for each other you need to be purposefully selfless. You need to give in areas that are not as important to you. It's a practice you should begin while you date and a habit you'll bring into your marriage.

Strength in relationship is found through selfless acts.

Communication Collapse

Communication should be so easy. At its' core it's just data in – data out. Unfortunately, we humans aren't computers and the data we seek to share gets all muddled up. We have a thought but fear stops us from speaking it, or has us minimizing the intended message. We choose to water down our words rather than risk a negative response.

And the words others speak to us move through our filters so that the original meaning is transformed. Even a simple word can have multiple meanings and a misinterpretation can send a conversation way off course. Then we assume things about the message received, rather than risk asking questions.

Miscommunications, misunderstandings, misinterpretations, inaccurate assumptions, hurts left unspoken, all add bricks to a wall between two people in a relationship.

Unfortunately, communication is the way that humans bond. The more muddled, the more opportunity for trouble in the relationship.

Just take a look through these Partnership Pitfalls. Overcoming any of them within the relationship requires good, honest communication through some possibly challenging conversations.

I believe that good communication is one of the most important keys to creating true and lasting love. Life will never be without challenge and you will need to maneuver through the ups, downs, twists and turns of life together with good and frequent communication.

As your relationship progresses, you need to feel confident in your ability to speak up and also to be heard. If your words fall on deaf ears that is a red flag that signals trouble.

And, of course, once words are spoken and commitments made you want to see that actions match words. Words of promise with no follow-up action ultimately have no meaning.

I always say that the goal is assertive communication. From a place of confidence you are able to say what you feel, ask for what you want, and

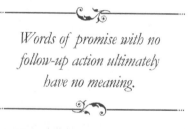

Words of promise with no follow-up action ultimately have no meaning.

truly hear what your significant other wishes to convey. You can work your way through tough conversations. Your sense of self-worth provides the armor to make it through.

Many miss the mark, falling instead into the main communication categories of passive, aggressive, or passive-aggressive.

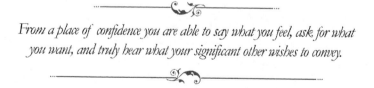

From a place of confidence you are able to say what you feel, ask for what you want, and truly hear what your significant other wishes to convey.

A passive communicator says very little. When they do speak it tends to be positive or agreeable. The main messages center around "I'm good," "I'm fine with that," "I just want what you want." People pleasers tend to be passive communicators. They need to feel that those around them are okay, in order to feel good themselves. So, they avoid speaking about anything that may make someone feel bad or uncomfortable. They just want everyone happy and will listen for clues about your mood. They rarely initiate any deep conversations. That generates too much fear.

While it can feel nice to be with someone so accommodating, the trouble with passive people is you can't really trust them. They say everything is fine, but is it really? If you end up in a relationship with a passive communicator you will likely find yourself guessing, worrying or living gloriously oblivious to the resentment your partner is generating. Sometimes the buildup will lead to a blow up.

When I describe people pleasing to clients, they are often surprised to hear that passive people are actually quite controlling. Their desire to have others happy has them manipulating and controlling conversations and outcomes to reach that end. Some will go to great lengths to avoid revealing the unpleasant.

You may find yourself trying to guess at what they really mean, taking action just in case.

An aggressive communicator, on the other hand, tends to always let their opinions be known. They will push their agenda and seek to be seen as right. This kind of person I call a people pusher. They too are controlling, but with a different goal in mind than the people pleaser. Instead of working to assure that others feel good, people pushers are all about themselves. Seldom do they consider the fallout of their words or actions as they push and maneuver to fulfill their needs. "I'm okay if I'm okay" is their battle cry.

With a passive aggressive communicator interactions can feel nicer but still focus on serving self. The underlying message is, "I'm going to get my way but I prefer that you feel at least somewhat good about it." Popular tactics used are guilt, omission of fact, misrepresenting the truth and outright lying.

When someone is a less than ideal communicator we tend to focus on the communication method much more than the message. For instance, if someone is aggressive or speaks too quickly, we may tend to discount everything they say.

Often the loudest, most aggressive communicators actually feel unheard. They end up victim to a self-fulfilling prophecy. They

Speak in love and listen with empathy

feel unheard, so they speak louder or longer and, as a result, they are ignored. So they try even harder to be heard by elevating the volume, and defenses against them increase even more.

I know it's hard, but I encourage you to try to focus on the message rather than the method. Perhaps you've been missing some nuggets. I would never suggest you take responsibility for your partner's communication challenges but you may be able to assist them. Truly hearing them beyond their deficiencies is a gift you can give out of love. You can, of course, at another time, address the aggression or other communication struggle and request that they work on assertive communication for the future.

Communication is key to working through any partnership pitfalls, so it is a cornerstone of a strong relationship. As you evaluate your relationship, take notice of whether you feel confident speaking out, and what his reactions are to the tough stuff.

Here is the most basic illustration of what must exist in your communication:

- You are confident to speak truth with love.

- He is willing to hear.

- He is confident to speak truth with love.

- You are willing to hear.

- Both are open to clarifying conversations to unveil facts.

- Both are willing to find a meeting of the minds and commit to any required action.

- Both have good follow through and execution of agreed upon actions.

You both need integrity with your words. Even the toughest conversations need to be had. Speak in love and listen with empathy. Seek to understand, create an action plan together, and then turn those actions into words.

Single Mom Moment: The Authoritative Tone

This communication challenge is not exclusive to single moms but....based on the experiences shared from many single moms I do believe it is a pattern and worthy of mention. I must admit that I have been guilty at times as well.

By the time you begin dating it is possible that you've been a single mom for years. It's been you and your kids. You are CEO, COO, President and Dictator in your home. You are in charge of those with which you dwell. You may make many, many requests throughout a day. You have much to do and too little time. There is a sense of urgency that requires immediate follow through often.

- Get your shoes on.

- Put those dishes in the sink,

- We need to leave in 10 minutes.

- Turn off the light and go to sleep.

- Put those in the dirty clothes bin, please.

As sole dictator and disciplinarian in your home there is a tone that may accompany those requests and an expectation of follow through. After all, you are the mom.

That tone can become habit and that role automatic.

In the dating world the same tone and expectation for follow through does not fit well.

Thus, this single mom moment seeks to alert you to the possibility that your tone, at times, may be more Drill Sargent than Soul Mate. Your date mate does not want a relationship that resembles the one you have with your kids. My guess is you aren't intending to come across as a dictator to others. It's just the habit you may have created by the role you've been in. So, please, mom, if this is you, watch your tone.

Commitment Concerns

Remember when I asked you to just "try new perspectives on for size"? Trying is testing the waters, seeing how things will feel. That is really what the start of any dating relationship is, right? You have little invested in the beginning. You're checking things out, trying the relationship on for size. Slowly, at each cross roads you decide whether to end it or move on to invest more and explore deeper.

At some point, if you are truly seeking your forever-someone, you both determine that you've tried and tested enough and move to the point of full commitment. In a relationship, commitment is the end of "try." It is your all-in promise. As Yoda so brilliantly remarked, "Do or do not...there is no try." I must agree with him.

Does your date mate have commitment concerns? Listen to what he says. If his stated goal is marriage are his actions consistent with those words? Is he introducing you to friends and family, including you in a vision for his future, even if only for a concert seven months out? Is he transitioning you into his life? Or, on the contrary, has he started looking for a house to buy without consulting you about any of it?

It is rare to change a man's mind. If he has commitment concerns they'll probably stay. Listen when he tells you he's not ready or it's not

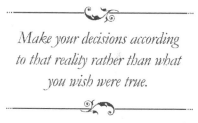

Make your decisions according to that reality rather than what you wish were true.

his desire and make your decisions according to that reality rather than what you wish were true.

Too often I see relationships progressing nicely to the brink of marriage and then something stalls it. For some women it is connection to a man who has stated his commitment concerns and a desire to keep things loose but she holds on "in case."

I've heard this or something similar from so many women.

- He doesn't want any long term commitment.

- He doesn't want to put a label on the relationship.

- He's not interested in monogamy.

- He doesn't want the pressure of family get-togethers.

- He's not ready to settle down right now but someday.

Followed by things like:

- We have so much fun together.

- He's lost without me.

- He helps me.

- We've tried breaking up but we end up missing each other too much and getting back together.

- He can't stand the thought of me dating anyone else. It really hurts him.

- I know he really loves me.

If this is you, you are in limbo land, dating with no commitment and no promise of it in the future. Again, if this is what you want it's all good, you are both on the same page. However, if you really want to love and be cherished, this man probably is not your path to that goal. If these are the kinds of phrases you are hearing, then he is getting what he wants from the relationship, but you are not. He's designing it and you are getting dragged along in eternal dating. Tim Keller, author of the book *"Meaning of Marriage"*, refers to this as the "faux spouse". One partner is getting all they want or need from the relationship without a full commitment.

If you truly are seeking your forever-someone then it won't happen unless the man you are dating wants that too. He needs to pursue you to that point, and he must want you and that commitment for himself – not because you coerced him into it.

In the Relentless Mistrust chapter, I wrote a bit about a previous relationship. He was the date mate I wanted to trust but couldn't. That relationship started as many do -- he wanted to see other people and communicated that clearly to me. I was dating one or two others a little bit too, but I made myself mostly available to him. I wanted to spend time with him. He was well-known in my circles as a playboy. In hindsight it is very clear to me that I was focused on the win. Getting him to commit would have been great validation of my self-worth, or so I thought at the time.

After a time he liked me, he liked me a lot. It was time to make my move. I threw the ultimatum at him. He had to date me exclusively or I was going to stop seeing him.

Well, he wanted to keep seeing me. So, he *told* me exactly what I wanted to hear. Yes, he would date only me. It was a huge victory for me. Except . . . my gut kept telling me not to trust him.

Eventually, after far more heartache than I should have endured, it became apparent that he was absolutely still seeing other people. He did want me, but on his terms. He would *tell* me anything to have what he wanted. He was not willing, however, to *do* just anything to keep what he wanted.

My awesomeness could not make his desire change. He wanted to date many and he would. I hadn't listened when he plainly shared his wishes.

Even if he hadn't cheated, his attitude should have sent me running to the hills. After *saying* he would date only me, he continually reminded me to appreciate the *sacrifice* he had made for me in giving up other women. I needed to show my gratitude . . . constantly.

The mindset you really want from your forever-someone is an appreciation for the gift they have received in you.

A man who's been captured or coerced into commitment, rather than willingly choosing it, may continue to feel he has sacrificed and that you owe him. Not a good foundation on which to create a partnership. It primes you for the scorecard or strings mentality.

A man who's been captured or coerced into commitment, rather than willingly choosing it, may continue to feel he has sacrificed and that you owe him.

Maybe you are the one with commitment concerns. The relationship has followed the appropriate path and he's starting to talk marriage, but something in your gut yells, "Stop!"

Is it a fear unrelated to him that must be healed within you before you move forward, or is there something about him that's got you feeling uncertain? Are there red flags you're trying to overlook? Is there something that you don't like about the way you are with him? Is the problem real or imagined? These are questions to ask and answer for yourself and for your relationship, and the answers may not be easy for you to accept. While I am not suggesting you rush through the final stages of dating to commit for life, limbo land can't last forever.

Perhaps you are what one single mom dubbed, a "runner". Your fight or flight urge kicks in at the first sign of trouble with a heavy emphasis on the flight response. You've been abandoned so many times that it's just an expectation. You don't commit. There's just more to separate and work through to end it so you prefer to keep things simple.

Lingering relationships present other types of commitment concerns you may need to examine before you are ready for a *True Love*. Lingering relationships are ones you know will go nowhere good, but just won't go away. These can wreak havoc, creating love triangles, shifting focus, stealing time and attention away from a mate with true potential.

Maybe you can't fully leave the relationship due to your own insecurity about finding someone else. You have fun, then fight, you break up and get back together every few weeks or months. Deep down you know this person is not right for you, but there is a comfort and security in knowing you have your fallback guy.

Or perhaps you are stuck on a man for his remodel potential. Sure, the relationship isn't what you want it to be now, but someday . . . You stay out of hope that he will make that change you want, and you can't seem to let it go. After all, you tell yourself, if he finally transforms then someone else will reap the reward of all the work you've put in. Soon, very soon he'll see . . .

Commitment might be elusive for other reasons. Maybe you're in a serious relationship that you know will not go anywhere, but haven't mustered the courage to have *that* conversation yet. It leaves you stuck and unavailable for your forever-someone.

Perhaps you've had a crush for months or years on someone you haven't even dated. He is your "what if" guy. You imagine what a relationship with him would be like, but have no idea whether that dream can come true. Meanwhile, your fairytale view is so exquisite and appealing to you that it is difficult for any *Real Man* to compete with it. So you dabble with dating some who can't ever compare to your dreamboat, while you hold out hope that one day he'll notice you on the elevator or at the gym.

Or maybe you aren't willing to let go of your friend-with-benefits, maybe because of the chemically induced pleasurable connection that keeps you coming back. In this scenario, you may say you are available for dating, but in fact you aren't able to fully commit to anyone else. You have not been able to break the bond.

What these lingering relationships all have in common is that they box off a little piece of the heart, erecting commitment barriers that leave you unable to give yourself fully to a new relationship.

Have you ever heard the story of Hernando Cortez? He was a Spanish Explorer who landed on the shores of Mexico in 1519 with his army, ready for a battle. There were difficult circumstances and he feared his men would retreat, so he ordered one of his leaders to go back to the beach to burn their boats. Why? Because limited options created an increased desire to succeed against the seemingly insurmountable odds. Limited options placed the army's full focus on standing their ground and fighting for survival, rather than running to the boats.

I am certainly not suggesting you treat your relationships like a battlefield, or that retreat should always be an option in dating. But when you visualize the soldier who appears intent on the battle, but who has one foot on the sand ready to jump into the boat, you can see that he is not all-in. The available options divide his attention.

A lingering relationship will do just that. It splits your focus and takes your time and attention away from pursuing what might be the real thing.

I'm not suggesting you can't play the field. Certainly you can date a few people at a time while there are no commitments to any one of them. Once you've concluded a relationship is not right for you, though, cut ties and let your heart move on.

Whether it's you or a date mate hanging on, lingering relationships will keep you from making the full commitment to a new person with true potential. Whether it's a friend-with-benefits scenario or a former flame that hasn't been fully extinguished, relationships with such loose ends will stand in the way of finding a committed relationship with your *True Love*.

Abuse

I've lived emotional abuse and am a survivor! I want to share some of the red flags I've learned to help you identify this kind of relationship and either steer clear or evaluate whether you might be in an abusive relationship now. From within, it is often difficult to see the signs objectively and trust your instincts. I'm not an expert, but what I believe based on my research and personal experience is that the strategies you would apply to a "normal" relationship work against you in an abusive relationship. An abusive relationship presents an entirely different set of concerns both in trying to leave it and in trying to heal for a better one.

Even in a healthy relationship you cannot expect perfection. However, there is a core truth that through your brokenness and missteps you are each authentically working to create a loving, respectful partnership. An abusive partner has a very different goal and that is to manipulate, control and tear down. They blame you for everything, and it comes from a sense of entitlement more than just a misalignment of responsibility.

Your vulnerabilities are turned on you like weapons to tear you down or hold you there. You don't realize initially. You think he's working towards a great partnership while in actuality his full focus is on control. He has a complete sense of entitlement that doesn't allow him to see the results of any of his actions. If you have a reaction to his abuse he will respond as if he was just skipping happily through the room, when you overreacted with a spontaneous outburst, or felt fear out of nowhere. To him it just becomes more proof that you are a drama queen. He will not see cause and effect.

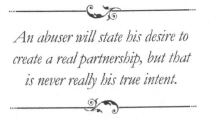

An abuser will state his desire to create a real partnership, but that is never really his true intent.

An abuser will state his desire to create a real partnership, but that is never really his true intent. He'll say the right things, providing just enough hope for you to stay longer than you should.

When I first met this particular significant other, he was so friendly and high energy. He laughed a lot and was very easy going. He seemed to really care about my happiness and supported my career. We were inseparable immediately. The verbal abuse started slowly and worsened over time, as is the norm.

I will never forget the day he yelled across the kitchen, "You're lucky I don't bash your head in right now!" By that point the abuse had been escalating for years and the truth was that part of me wanted him to beat me up. Then there would *finally* be evidence to show what was really happening to me, external proof of the pain I was feeling on the inside. A black eye gives your secrets away and makes the abuse more real, while emotional scars are buried deep.

As I look back, it was glimmers of hope that kept me stuck in that relationship for as long as I was. He knew to keep me stringing along on at least a few. That is one of the strategies abusers use. I was in this environment of utter chaos with no predictability, and had this tendency to disregard the bad stuff after it happened and instead key in on the

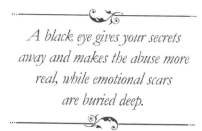

A black eye gives your secrets away and makes the abuse more real, while emotional scars are buried deep.

little things that I felt were signs of positive change. He would write me a letter of apology, telling me how much he loved me. He would promise to work together with me to make everything better.

I would forget to look for substantive, sustainable change. Without consistency, the positive stuff can have no lasting impact. If it lasts even three months and then reverts back to yuck you are still in yuck. He can't stop being the guy he really is, so despite the intermittent good-guy appearances, you won't ever really know which guy is going to walk through the door in a moment, and you never know what the day's grievance will be.

I didn't want to give up on a relationship prematurely. I kept thinking that we'd be able to work it out. I continued to wrongly believe, "He loves me and I love him. We are partners".

As the abuse ramped up, my expectations for the relationship slowly eroded. Smaller and smaller positive incidents became even more important. The backwardness of this didn't hit me until I caught myself telling a friend, "Yes, but at least he doesn't hit me."

Since when does this become the bar to shoot for??

I got so focused on the little glimmers that I lost sight of what *I* wanted in a relationship. I forgot to pay attention to his actions and not just his words. Words take just a few seconds to say, and are not what shapes the experience of your life.

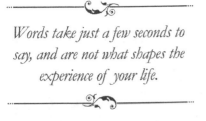

Words take just a few seconds to say, and are not what shapes the experience of your life.

The trend was for him to blow up or rage. Sometimes it was over quickly, other times it went on for weeks. Then he would come back with kind words out of remorse, "I love you. We'll work this out. I'm sorry." I'd feel that glimmer of hope and think, "He really gets it this time. Now things will be different."

But the words were said and gone in the blink of an eye, a thought that passed through his mind and over lips or from pen to paper in ink and nothing more. I kept the written words of apology and endearment in a drawer by my bed like trophies. They were prized possessions to me. To him they were like handcuffs, the instruments that held me where I was.

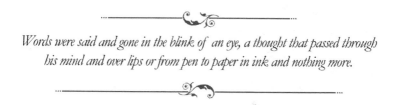

Words were said and gone in the blink of an eye, a thought that passed through his mind and over lips or from pen to paper in ink and nothing more.

Is there rehabilitation for abusers? There have been some positive results reported, but according to what I've read, any success stories are few and far between. If there are signs of any kind of abuse in your partnership this is more than a pitfall!

Domestic violence encompasses a spectrum of behaviors that abusers use to control victims. The following list includes warning signs that someone may be abusive. This list is compiled from two sources, the National Network to End Domestic Violence (nnedv.org) and the National Domestic Violence Hotline (thehotline.org).

"Red flags" include someone who:

- Wants to move too quickly into the relationship

- Early in the relationship flatters you constantly, and seems "too good to be true."

- Wants you all to him- or herself; insists that you stop spending time with your friends or family

- Insists that you stop participating in hobbies or activities, quit school, or quit your job

- Does not honor your boundaries

- Is excessively jealous and accuses you of being unfaithful

- Wants to know where you are all of the time and frequently calls, emails, and texts you throughout the day

- Criticizes or puts you down; says you are crazy, stupid, and/or fat/unattractive, or that no one else would ever want or love you

- Takes no responsibility for his or her behavior and blames others.

- Has a history of abusing others

- Blames the entire failure of previous relationships on his or her former partner; for example, "My ex was totally crazy."

- Takes your money or runs up your credit card debt

- Rages out of control with you but can maintain composure around others

- Tells you that you can never do anything right

- Keeping you or discouraging you from seeing friends

or family members

- Embarrasses or shames you with put-downs
- Controls every penny spent in the household
- Takes your money or refuses to give you money for expenses
- Looks at you or acts in ways that scare you
- Controls who you see, where you go, or what you do
- Prevents you from making your own decisions
- Tells you that you are a bad parent or threatens to harm or take away your children
- Destroys your property or threatens to hurt or kill your pets
- Intimidates you with guns, knives or other weapons
- Pressures you to have sex when you don't want to or to do things sexually you're not comfortable with
- Pressures you to use drugs or alcohol

Abuse is never the fault of the victim and it can be hard to end an abusive relationship for many reasons, including safety. If you experience these "red flags," you can confide in a friend or reach out for support from a domestic violence advocate. If you believe a friend or relative is being abused, offer your nonjudgmental support and help.

For help and information: National Domestic Violence Hotline: 1-800-799-SAFE (7233) or TTY 1-800-787-3224

If you think you might be in an abusive relationship right now I urge you to find additional resources in your area.

You should also check out the Aspire News App for your phone. It has a wealth of resources and hidden alert system you can use to contact friends, family and/or 911 if you get into a dangerous situation.

Pondering from Dating to I Do

Many begin as little girls to envision a future and that one big day. The white dress, the handsome man in the tux, the wedding and reception. How many hours are logged dreaming during play with Barbie and Ken dolls? The people who named their dwelling Barbie's Dream House were spot on. The importance some women attach to the day itself and all that surrounds it is almost as intense as Olympic training. The reality show, "Bridezilla," captures the frantic and emotional high-stakes of the near culmination of every fantasy its contestants have had since they were young girls.

As you begin to ponder a shift from Dating to I Do, avoid a preoccupation with the idea of marrying before a certain age or crossing the finish line before a specific date. My dad always says, "It's not a game of musical chairs, " Too many jump at the one they are with when the time is right rather than waiting for the right one. "Whelp, it's time and you're here. Let's do this!"

Avoid the trappings of a focus on the big party to happen on your special day. Instead, set your sights beyond the one big day to a lifetime with your love. Marriage can be wonderful, but takes work. Much more work than the wedding day. Do not make the decision lightly. Marriage can't be about one day. It is about the life that follows.

Marriage is the ultimate commitment and there is much to ponder. I don't know that anyone enters this decision phase without some amount of confusion and fear. It's a big step and none of us has a crystal ball to tell us what a future holds. By this point there is usually quite an investment of time and two hearts almost all-in. Will two lives fit to blend as one?

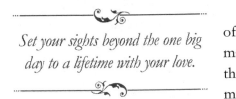

Set your sights beyond the one big day to a lifetime with your love.

Eric and I spent a lot of time discussing marriage before we made the leap to I Do. A marriage to me would mean big changes for him. I had two kids, a house, material stuff and personal baggage. There was a lot of responsibility and some messiness to my life. He had lived more simply prior to meeting me. Would he be ready to jump in full force? I knew first hand that a marriage relationship was not an instant fairy tale. I was fearful and resistant for a time. Would Eric and I be able to navigate life's challenges well together once we were all in? Could I trust and fully give my heart away again? Was he finally my forever-someone?

Tim Keller, in his book *"Meaning of Marriage"*, describes marriage this way, "Marriage is glorious but hard. It's a burning joy and strength, and yet it is also blood, sweat, and tears, humbling defeats and exhausting victories." (p. 21) He goes on to explain that each member of the union is broken, flawed and selfish. How could it be anything but hard? "Raw natural talent does not enable you to play baseball as a pro or write great literature without enduring discipline and enormous work. Why would it be easy to live lovingly and well with another human being in light of what is profoundly wrong within our human nature?" *(p 40)*

Mr. Keller then goes on to share that we have no way of *really* knowing who we are marrying because the act itself changes us. Time creates opportunity for growth, new interests and goals, transitions in a career. Your forever-someone will change over time and so will you.

But living life in partnership with each other creates the promise of an opportunity to learn and grow together.

As we commune with our love, as we seek to grow and become better, we have the opportunity to work through more of our hurts in a union that pits us with someone who is also broken and hurting, but committed to health and partnership. I say this not to scare you, but to give you pause.

📖 *17 As iron sharpens iron, so one person sharpens another. (Proverbs 27:17)*

The time you spend with your date mate gives you a moments in time view of who he is and who you are with him. There is time to experience the ups and downs of life, and hopefully many deep talks sharing hurts and hopes.

> *Commitment is purposeful and communicates a tenacious promise.*

Commitment is purposeful and communicates a tenacious promise. You feel it. Your commitment is a pledge to both yourself and to your significant other. And true commitment is key. A commitment to your forever-someone to stick through the work of loving one another, the missteps of healing as you bristle, is beautiful and tough. It is a promise to choose selflessness over selfishness over and over and daily. Not with strings attached, but because by committing to a marriage where one serves the other you create the upward momentum of sustainable partnership and love.

> *"For this reason a man will leave his father and mother and be united to his wife, and the two will become one flesh.* [32] *This is a profound mystery….." (Ephesians 5:31-32)*

As I've said before, I don't believe selflessness is innate for any of us. Without an intentional commitment to and focus on serving one another, each spouse in a partnership will become disenchanted. You will complain, "Wow, is he selfish!" while your significant other screams the same, either within or out loud.

And when your spouse lets you down, as he absolutely will, knowing that you are loved already will be key. Feeling God's love first will leave your tank full. You don't have to depend on your spouse for a love he may not be able to give.

So when, as a couple, you start exploring the move from

Dating to I Do, I encourage you to think long and hard. Be objective. Weigh the pros and cons. Consider the list you made as you created your vision of the one. Appreciate the strengths. Assess any red flags or flaws.

The list in the Partnership Pitfalls doesn't cover every challenge a couple might face but will give you plenty to ponder as you evaluate. It's not necessarily about assuring that the relationship has none of the trip-ups, but more importantly it is about how each of you have handled discussions about them. Do you each feel confident enough to initiate tough topics? Were each of you able to communicate without getting defensive, has there been commitment towards change and specific growth strategies designed and started? Do you each own your brokenness and flaws? No relationship is going to be without challenge, but your ability to communicate about those challenges will be key to its success.

Look at the entire picture. Pull those rose colored glasses off and try to see the balance of the good and bad. Turning a blind eye to either can be problematic.

How are you as a couple? Do you work better together than you do individually? Do your personalities, strengths and weaknesses complement one another? Have you met his family and friends? Have you had a meeting of the minds on the most important topics? Do you have a strong set of paired values? Are your plans for a future together aligned? Do you see well beyond the excitement of the wedding day? Are you friends plus?

To stand the test of time, your relationship must be based on more than physical attraction or an attachment to status and financial security. It must be a friendship built from common interests, trust, and an ability to share intimate ideas without fear.

As you evaluate the relationship, are you coming from a place of strength? Do you know from your core that you are fine with or without him? From this place you can make an objective decision.

- Don't allow neediness to color your decision.

- Don't focus on the "if only" version of him. How do you feel about him as he is?

- Don't place emphasis on keeping him off the market so no one else can have him.

- Don't focus on how this relationship validates you.

And if it is your practice or you are open to trying, pray. Ask God for discernment and wisdom. Ask Him to reveal His plan for your future with this man. Are you to take life lessons and move on, or is he to be your forever-someone?

Remember, you are not looking for just someone you are looking for *the* one. If you do the work, and do it well, you too can feel like the luckiest woman in the world. You can feel loved and cherished for a lifetime.

After much pondering, our Dating to I Do transition was wonderful. During our wedding vows Eric hesitated. The

Pastor looked at him questioningly. Eric chuckled apologetically for the pause and said, "I got lost in her eyes." The pastor responded with, "Isn't that awesome!" It was a very sweet moment. Afterwards, as my Maid of Honor gave her toast, she shared that, to her, the moment symbolized our relationship from the start. She said, "They've been lost in each other's eyes since they met!"

We involved my two boys in our ceremony. We were creating more than a marriage between two people, we were cementing a family. Eric made a commitment to them during our ceremony as well as to me. We presented each of them with a family medallion. While our rings symbolized our connection as husband and wife, these medallions served as a physical representation of our connection to one another as a family.

We included them in our pouring of the sand ritual as well. This practice is fairly new and replaces the lighting of the unity candle in some marriage ceremonies. Eric and I began by pouring colored sand together into the bottom of the container, he orange and I purple. This symbolized our union as husband and wife but also the foundation that we would create together in our home. Once that was complete the four of us added a second layer that signified the creation of our family.

As we poured, my brother accompanied the soloist, who sang, "Bless the Broken Road," co-written by Marcus Hummon, Bobby Boyd, and Jeff Hanna. It was a beautiful moment and tears of joy and delight streamed down my face. It was a very appropriate song, especially for me. It had been a long journey with many missteps and much heartache but we were blessed and I had married my *True Love*.

Not an End but a Beginning.......

The book has come to an end but for you this is just the beginning. My hope is that this book has helped you to see the possibility of *True Love* for yourself. You have read it to prepare and shared your plans with your CARE Group, or you have actually begun using learned strategies in new or existing relationships, also perhaps with the support of your CARE Group. I expect that you've created solid relationships through your CARE Group and that they will remain as sounding boards and continue to provide perspective. I hope that you will feel more empowered in dating situations. I hope that you fully believe or are working to believe to your core that you are loved and cherished regardless of what any man thinks of you.

You are wonderfully made and have value beyond your imagination. You are worthy of *True Love*.

If you have not invited Him into your life, God sits waiting. If you have never done so, inviting God into your life requires a simple prayer. *"Dear God, I know that you sent Jesus to be my Savior, and that He died on the cross for my sins. Please forgive me of all of my sins, and come into my life and change me. In Jesus' Name, Amen."*

> *⁹ If you declare with your mouth, "Jesus is Lord," and believe in your heart that God raised him from the dead, you will be saved. (Romans 10:9)*

You are wonderfully made and have value beyond your imagination.

You are worthy of True Love.

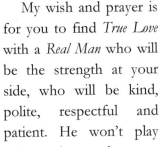

My wish and prayer is for you to find *True Love* with a *Real Man* who will be the strength at your side, who will be kind, polite, respectful and patient. He won't play games or keep you guessing. He will let you know where you stand and how he feels with both his words and actions. He will have integrity, so those words and actions match. He will seek to protect all of you; your mind, heart, spirit, soul and body. His goal will be partnership, never manipulation or control. He will listen without defensiveness and seek to fully understand. He will lift you up, not tear you down. He'll give you grace without being a pushover. The perfect blend of loving all of who you are with the ability to kindly and gently call you on your stuff. He will be strong and confident but not overpowering and have a focus on serving others over getting his own needs met. He will have a heart of gold and a love for God.

And, ultimately, he will help you feel loved and cherished, until death do you part.

Acknowledgements

First and foremost I must say thank you to my wonderful husband, Eric. I will never find the words to express my appreciation for you. It is our relationship and the way you cherish me that provide me with the opportunity to write a book like this. You are my inspiration and my greatest encourager. We get to share great joy, love, laughter and adventure on a daily basis! I'm so blessed to be on God's great journey with you!

And to my two beautiful boys, you are the reason for all that I do. I've had the privilege of being your mom and watching you grow into fine young men. I look forward to seeing what your futures hold.

This book is dedicated to the many wonderful singles and single moms who have shared their hearts and hurts with me. They have allowed me into their world and invited me along their journey. They have been courageous, vulnerable and willing to do what it takes.

They have engaged in the pursuit of True Love.

Bibliography

The Holy Bible, New International Version®, NIV® Copyright © 1973, 1978, 1984, 2011 by Biblica, Inc.®

Daniel Amen, M.D., *Change Your Brain Change Your Life,* (Harmony, 1998)

Laura Sessions Stepp, *Unhooked: How Young Women Pursue Sex, Delay Love and Lose at Both* (Riverhead Books, 2008)

"Walking Her Home," by Mark Schultz from *Broken and Beautiful – Expanded Edition* (Word Records, 2007)

Timothy Keller with Kathy Keller, *The Meaning of Marriage: Facing the Complexities of Commitment with the Wisdom of God* (Dutton, 2011)

William F. Harley, Jr. and Fleming H. Revell, *His Needs Her Needs: Building an Affair Proof Marriage* (Revell, 2001)

⌒ ABOUT KIRSTEN ⌒

Kirsten E. Vogel openly admits that she has made many dating mistakes over the years and has endured many negative relationship experiences, including abuse. Yet, she yearned for true love and partnership and was committed to healing.

After working through her hurts and dating as a single mom, she is now gloriously and happily married to Eric and feels like one of the luckiest women in the world. Her mission is for every woman to experience the kind of love she shares.

Through her work as CEO of Focus Forward Coaching, LLC and also her volunteer endeavors, Kirsten has had the privilege of supporting many individuals through their relationship challenges.

She has authored two leadership books *Defeat the Drama* and *From People Problems to Productivity*. She has also been featured as an expert for media such as: *NBC Nightly News, Fox 2 News, National Public Radio* and for publications such as *Entrepreneur Magazine, Fox Business* and *Fitness Magazine*.

She has been a member of the National Speakers' Association since 2010. Her workshops and keynote addresses are rich with proven strategies that can be implemented immediately to enact change in life and work. Her fun and high-energy style has received rave reviews from participants who often marvel at her ability to simplify complex information while making the event entertaining. She is adept at injecting stories to increase motivation and anchor learning.

Kirsten is available for speaking or participation in your event and for Coaching. Contact her here:
Kirsten E. Vogel (Ross), MLIR, SPHR
248-973-7595
www.FocusForwardCoaching.com
DefeatTheDrama.com
info@DefeatTheDrama.com

Find the Companion Workbook by visiting:
ToLoveAndBeCherished.com/Products